A Song for Ireland

Mary —

love —

Bob.

Christmas 1982

A Song for Ireland

Mary O'Hara

MICHAEL JOSEPH
LONDON

First published in Great Britain by
Michael Joseph Limited
44 Bedford Square
London W.C.1.
1982

© Mary O'Hara 1982

ISBN 0 7181 2161 9

Printed and bound in Great Britain
by Fakenham Press Limited, Fakenham, Norfolk

Songs

ACKNOWLEDGMENTS

I am indebted to the many friends who, over the years, have encouraged me to persevere with the singing of Irish songs. These songs always have been and always will be the core of my work.

With regard to this present book, I want especially to thank Dr Padraig O'Toole who helped me with the research, and John Paddy Browne who read the typescript and offered much helpful advice. He also contributed the 'Notes on the Structure of Irish Songs' which appear at the end of the book.

I thank Thomas Wolfangel of Dublin, the fashion designer, whose patience in selecting outfits for my various photographic excursions into Ireland was seldom rewarded due to the vagaries of the Irish weather. And I thank Mournecraft Ltd of Rostrevor, Co. Down, who made the harp that appears on the jacket and in many of the photographs in the book.

Finally I would like to express my thanks and appreciation to all those listed below, who have between them contributed the many lovely pictures appearing in my book: Bodleian Library, Oxford; Bill Doyle; Bobbie Hanvey; Richard Haughton; Sarah Hook; Irish Tourist Board of Dublin; Liam Lyons; Northern Irish Tourist Board, Belfast; Rex Roberts; Spectrum Colour Library; Stuart Sadd. These photographs are of course their Copyright.

The words of the following songs are reprinted by kind permission of Boosey & Hawkes Music Publishers Ltd: PADRAIG THE FIDDLER © 1919 by Boosey & Co.; I KNOW WHERE I'M GOING, THE GARTEN MOTHER'S LULLABY, SHE MOVED THROUGH THE FAIR, THE NEXT MARKET DAY from 'Irish Country Songs' (Herbert Hughes) © 1909 by Boosey & Co. The following are also available in sheet music: THE LARK IN THE CLEAR AIR (Oxford University Press), SCORN NOT HIS SIMPLICITY (Eaton Music).

DOWN BY THE SALLY GARDENS and THE STOLEN CHILD by W. B. Yeats are reproduced by kind permission of Macmillan Publishers; THE SONG OF GLENDUN by kind permission of Blackwood & Sons Ltd; and SCORN NOT HIS SIMPLICITY by kind permission of the song-writer.

The author and publishers express their hope to have duly acknowledged all contributions in this book.

Introduction

A Sense of Ireland

Mary O'Hara's Ireland is the title of one of my earliest albums. The songs on that album form a cross-section of what appeals to me in the Irish musical tradition and so I find little difficulty relating to the vision of Ireland portrayed by those songs. However, when the same title, 'Mary O'Hara's Ireland', was suggested for this book I felt some reluctance. Somehow I imagined that one should be more objective about one's country than about one's songs. I was keenly aware of the many gaps in my knowledge about Ireland and, though I love the country as much as her songs, I felt I did not know it well enough to write a book. Then, again, I thought, why shouldn't I be as subjective about my country as I am about my songs? Was it possible, I asked myself, for anyone to have an objective view of his or her own country? Was such a view even desirable? There are as many Irelands as there are people with images of Ireland and each person's Ireland is as unique as each one's personal experience.

The Ireland I try to portray in this book is the Ireland of my songs – hence the title: *A Song for Ireland*. If there are aspects of *your* Ireland missing from this book, it's what one might expect because it's *my* Ireland. One can argue that song does not always project a realistic image of a country, and that may be true. Mountains can become more majestic and valleys greener; running streams sound more melodious, ancient rocks seem more mysterious and ruined castles more roman-tic. In song, the people too can take on new characteristics and history-shaping events may be viewed through the rose-tinted spectacles of the dreamer. Some-times, indeed, the Ireland of the exile is more attractive than the real one, but I have no quarrel with that. For most of my life, circumstances have made me an exile from the land where I was born. Yet this land follows me wherever I go. I carry it round in my head. My own biography, no doubt, has coloured my consciousness of Ireland: my early childhood days in Sligo in the west of Ireland, my teenage and school days in Dublin, my singing, my marriage, my widow-hood and my lengthy sojourn in an English monastic community. These events have shaped the way I see my country and the way I feel about it.

During the writing of this book, I reviewed (and reminisced about) the 200 odd songs in my repertoire that I have been singing for many years in my

---

OPPOSITE *Mary O'Hara outside Kylemore Abbey, a Benedictine monastery set in the middle of the Connemara mountains in the west of Ireland. Mary spent 12 years of her life as a member of the Benedictine community at Stanbrook Abbey in England.*

concerts all over the world. I took a representative selection of these songs and I treated them as if they were a concert programme. Just as in my earlier concerts I presented the songs in groups depending on their themes, so, here, I have divided the book into various chapters, with the songs under the following headings: love, history, myth and the supernatural, lullaby and children, fairday and market, humour, lament, nature, and, finally, exile. These are the themes that predominate in my repertoire as far as my Songs of Ireland are concerned. It's a matter of opinion whether some songs belong to one category or another and the format adopted does not lend itself to any sort of chronological presentation, even if I thought it desirable. I did, however, make an attempt to intersperse Gaelic songs throughout the book. My favourite song in each category heads the chapters.

Until the middle of the last century, Gaelic was the spoken language of the majority of the Irish and there was a remarkable variety of popular poetry and music in the country. I've always thought it interesting that the old Gaelic musicians and scholars regarded all music as falling naturally into three categories: *suantrai*, music to make one sleep; *geantrai*, music to make one laugh, and *gultrai*, music to make one weep. Irish music has certainly done all these things for me, but not always for reasons that scholars would appreciate. However, there are many learned books on the subject of Irish music and song and anyone interested in further scholarly studies will find reference to these in the bibliography. Some of these books are valuable sources of information and are my constant companions.

This book, then, is neither a tourist guide nor an historical treatise on the music of Ireland: it is an anthology of my favourite Irish songs, those songs that I've liked well enough to sing in my concerts. It's a very selective, even subjective, view of Ireland, of my songs of Ireland, and of the associations these songs have for me and of the memories they evoke in me. It's not even my complete vision of Ireland because of the limitations imposed by the book's format. The accompanying photographs clothe the words of the poets in visual imagery, which for me makes this excursion into roots even more pleasurable. I hope that you, too, will find the journey stimulating.

OPPOSITE *Ben Bulben, a familiar view from my childhood home at the edge of Sligo harbour. It was at Ben Bulben that Diarmuid, hero of the epic Irish love saga 'The Pursuit of Diarmuid and Grainne' met his death while hunting wild boar. W. B. Yeats has immortalised the mountain in his poem 'Under Ben Bulben'. The epitaph on his tombstone is taken from the last lines of the same poem:*

Cast a cold eye
On life, on death
Horseman, pass by!

Chapter I

My Lagan Love

Where Lagan stream sings lullaby
There blows a lily fair;
The twilight gleam is in her eye
The night is on her hair.
And like a love-sick *leanán sídhe*
She hath my heart in thrall,
Nor life I owe nor liberty
For love is lord of all.

And often when the beetles' horn
Hath lulled the eve to sleep,
I steal unto her shieling lorn
And through the dooring peep.
There, on the crickets' singing stone
She spares the bogwood fire,
And hums in sad sweet undertone,
The song of heart's desire.

Love is a predominant theme in the songs of all peoples. This is hardly surprising for, through the ages, poets and song writers of every culture have shown love to be a constant preoccupation. Love, as the saying goes, does indeed make the world go round. Without its ecstasy and pain, its difficulties and delights, our world would be a dreary, if not an impossible, place in which to live. Search any song and somewhere in it you'll find a passage on this strongest of emotions. I begin this book with a chapter on 'being-in-love' songs. The unusually large corpus of Gaelic and Anglo-Irish vocal music has an abundance of rich and beautiful being-in-love songs, very often laced with references to nature. The Gael was vividly conscious of the natural world which I find splendidly refreshing. One might be forgiven for thinking that most of our songs are about war and rebellion because of Ireland's turbulent history, but, happily, this is not so.

Adorno claims that forms of art reflect the history of man more truthfully than any document; and, in Ireland's musical heritage, we find much that illuminates the soul as well as the history of our people. In Gaelic love-songs, particularly, there is a deep passionate sincerity and a tenderness of expression that is exceptionally beautiful. Five of the twenty songs I've chosen for this chapter have at least one verse in Gaelic. It was not easy to decide which songs to include in this section because there are so many in my repertoire that could be classified as love songs. So, I have been quite arbitrary in my selection and included obvious love songs like 'The Bonny Boy' under 'sorrow' instead of love because this is what it suggests to me.

The Lagan is that well-known river on which Belfast is built and so people are apt to assume that 'My Lagan Love' comes from County Antrim in the north-east corner of Ireland. However, some argue that the Lagan in the song refers to a stream that empties into Lough Swilly in County Donegal, not far from Letterkenny, where Herbert Hughes collected the song in 1903. Hughes first heard the tune played on a fiddle and traced it back to a sapper of the Royal Engineers working in Donegal in 1870 with the Ordnance Survey of Ireland. Though both Donegal and Antrim hold rich childhood memories for me, I have always associated the song with Belfast and its environs.

When I was a very small child my family used to spend summer holidays in the seaside town of Ballycastle on the north Antrim coast where the famous Lammas Fair (celebrated in song) took place. Today on the seafront is a memorial to Guglielmo Marconi, the inventor of wireless telegraphy, who made his first successful transmission between Ballycastle and Rathlin Island, six miles off the coast, almost 100 years ago. Many is the stroll we children had along Fair Head a few miles east of Ballycastle. This is the north-eastern extremity of Ireland, and it was a great thing for us, who had never yet set foot outside Ireland, to see Scotland and the islands from the top of Fair Head. Another spot which the family visited was the Giant's Causeway, that geological curiosity which is immortalised in Gaelic folklore and mythology.

I have happy memories of those days, as indeed I have of later and more recent visits to Northern Ireland giving concerts to remarkably receptive audiences in Belfast. I like visiting the city, if only to stay with my friends Samuel Crooks (the well-loved dean of Belfast Cathedral) and his vivacious wife, Isobel; their household is always full of laughter and good cheer. The last time I visited Belfast, I spent a couple of hours walking with a friend along the banks of the River Lagan which was the very picture of peace and quiet in the morning mist.

The words of 'My Lagan Love' were written by Seósamh Mac Cathmhaoil, who also wrote the words to 'The Gartan Mother's Lullaby', which I have included in Chapter IV. The melody of 'My Lagan Love' is traditional, and in the last century was played to the words of 'The Belfast Maid', a song which is now lost. I sing the majestic Hamilton Harty arrangement of 'My Lagan Love'. As a combination of exquisite lyric and noble air, the song, though not technically a 'folk song', must be admitted to that genre which some people call the 'high songs' of Ireland, or *amhrán mór*, in Gaelic.

This picture evokes memories of wet mornings during childhood holidays by the sea with the hope of sunshine breaking through later.

The *leanán sídhe* (fairy mistress) mentioned in the song is a malicious figure who frequently crops up in Gaelic love stories. One could call her the *femme fatale* of Gaelic folklore. She sought the love of men; if they refused, she became their slave, but if they consented, they became her slaves and could only escape by finding another to take their place. She fed off them and so her lovers gradually wasted away – a common enough theme in Gaelic medieval poetry, which often saw love as a kind of sickness. Most Gaelic poets in the past had their *leanán sídhe* to give them inspiration. This malignant fairy was for them a sort of Gaelic muse. On the other hand, the crickets mentioned in the song were a sign of good luck and their sound on the hearth a good omen. It was the custom of newly-married couples about to set up home to bring crickets from the hearths of their parents' house and place them in the new hearth.

'There on the crickets' singing stone
She spares the bogwood fire'.

Cucúin

Cucúin, a chuaichín,
    cá ndéanfaim a' samhradh?
    cá ndéanfaim a' samhradh?
Cucúin, a chuaichín,
    déanfam ins na gleannta é.
    déanfam ins na gleannta é.

Cucúin, a chuaichín,
    cé gheóbhadh 'nár dteannta ann?
    cé gheobhadh 'nár dteannta ann?
Cucúin, a chuaichín,
    beidh an dreóilín is a chlann ann.
    beidh an dreóilín is a chlann ann.

Cucúin, a chuaichín,
    cad a bheidh ann dúinn?
    cad a bheidh ann dúinn?
Cucúin, a chuaichín,
    beidh mil agus leamhnacht.
    beidh mil agus leamhnacht.

Cucúin, a chuaichín,
    an baol dúinn an seabhac ann?
    an baol dúinn an seabhac ann?
Cucúin, a chuaichín,
    ealóchaimid faoi chrann uaidh.
    ealóchaimid faoi chrann uaidh.

Cuckoo

Cuckoo, little cuckoo,
    where shall we spend the summer?
    where shall we spend the summer?
Cuckoo, little cuckoo,
    we'll spend it in the glens,
    we'll spend it in the glens.

Cuckoo, little cuckoo,
    who shall accompany us there?
    who shall accompany us there?
Cuckoo, little cuckoo,
    the wren and his children will be there,
    the wren and his children will be there.

Cuckoo, little cuckoo,
    what shall we find there?
    what shall we find there?
Cuckoo, little cuckoo,
    we'll find honey and milk there,
    we'll find honey and milk there.

Cuckoo, little cuckoo,
    will we be in danger from the hawk there?
    will we be in danger from the hawk there?
Cuckoo, little cuckoo,
    we'll escape from him under a tree,
    we'll escape from him under a tree.

This song is typical of the Gaelic song-writers' successful blending of love and nature themes. Taken at face value, the song seems to be nothing more than an innocent conversation between two little cuckoos, debating where best to spend the summer season but, in truth, the song is the secret language of two people planning to elope. They talk about their future life-style and the need to go unrecognised in their hideaway. The lovers will go to the glens and live obscure lives among other ordinary humble folk (the wrens), supported by love (honey) and milk (health foods!), safe from all possible enemies.

A Ballynure Ballad

As I was goin' to Ballynure, the day I well remember,
For to view the lads and lasses on the fifth day of November,
With a maring-doo-a-day, with a maring-doo-a-dad-dyio.

As I was going along the road, when homeward I was walking,
I heard a wee lad behind a ditch-a to his wee lass was talking,
With a maring-doo-a-day, with a maring-doo-a-dad-dyio.

Said the wee lad to the wee lass, 'Its will ye let me kiss ye,
For it's I have got the cordial eye that far exceeds the whiskey.'
With a maring-doo-a-day, with a maring-doo-a-dad-dyio.

This cordial that ye talk about, there's very few of them gets it,
For there it's nothing now but crooked combs and muslin gowns can catch it.
With a maring-doo-a-day, with a maring-doo-a-dad-dyio.

As I was goin' along the road, as homeward I was walking,
I heard a wee lad behind a ditch-a to his wee lass was talking.
With a maring-doo-a-day, with a maring doo-a-dad-dyio.

'A Ballynure Ballad' appears in Hughes' *Irish Country Songs* (1909) and is described as coming from County Antrim. The song probably dates from mid-nineteenth century, though the melody may be much older. I have always thought that the 'fifth day of November' referred to one of those hiring days common throughout the British Isles before the First World War. (There is a good description of a hiring fair in Thomas Hardy's *Far From the Madding Crowd*.) Other hiring songs seem to suggest that May was the month for the hiring fairs, where young boys and girls were hired out to employers who kept them for a year or more in return for a small fee, food and lodging. Though many of the hirings songs sound jolly, I'm sure that the lot of those hired was seldom so, but better, perhaps, than the lot of those not hired at all.

Ballynure is in County Antrim and was the scene of the wake of William Orr, one of the Presbyterian leaders of the United Irishmen, who was executed in 1797. The wake was held in the Presbyterian Meeting House in the village. A few miles away is Ballyeaston, the home of United States President Andrew Johnson's grandfather, who emigrated to America in about 1750.

The quiet of dusk on an Irish hillside.

Calen O Custure Me

1. When as I view your comely grace
       Calen o custure me,
    Your golden haires, your angel's face,
       Calen o custure me.

2. Your coral lips, your crimson cheeks,
       Calen o custure me,
    That Gods and men both love and like,
       Calen o custure me.

3. My soul with silence moving sense
       Calen o custure me,
    Doth wish of God with reverence,
       Calen o custure me.

4. Long life and vertue you possesse,
       Calen o custure me,
    To match those gifts of worthinesse,
       Calen o custure me.

5. Then how dare I with boldened face
       Calen o custure me,
    Presume to wish or crave your face,
       Calen o custure me.

I first came to know and love this song in a rather roundabout manner. I've long admired the work of that highly-skilled musician Grainne Yeats and, in my early singing days, we were in touch over a recording contract she had been offered. Then I gave up singing and went into a monastery for twelve silent years. As soon as I came out of the monastery, I searched for Grainne's album and, when I failed to find it, contacted her again. She very kindly sent me an album of hers made in Japan and it was on this record that I heard 'Calen O' for the first time. I have been singing it ever since, together with Schubert's 'Wiegenlied', another gem from the same album.

'Calen O Custure Me' has a most curious history and in a sense is only partly Irish. The jumble 'Calen o custure me' is found in Shakespeare's *Henry V* and is a phonetic rendering of what appears to be an old Gaelic song, now lost. The Gaelic song *'Cailín ó Chois tSiúire Mé'* (I am a girl from beside the river Suir) is referred to in a poem found in a late seventeenth-century manuscript from County Fermanagh: the poet complains that singing such songs would be a more profitable occupation for him than writing poetry. There is reference to 'Calen o custure me' in an English publication entitled, *A Handeful of Pleasant Delites* (1584), and also in a manuscript called *William Ballet's Lute Book*, now in the library of Trinity College, Dublin. This manuscript is said to have belonged to King James VI of Scotland and dates probably not later than 1600. In Shakespeare's *Henry V* (IV, 4), Ensign Pistol throws the phrase at his French prisoner on the battlefield of Agincourt:

> French prisoner: *Je pense que vous êtes le gentilhomme de bonne qualité.*
> Pistol: Quality? Calen o custure me! art thou a gentleman?

Beyond that, we don't know what Pistol, or for that matter Shakespeare, made of the Gaelic phrase. Probably nothing.

The version of 'Calen O Custure Me' that I sing is taken from *A Handeful of Pleasant Delites*, where the song appears as twenty-one couplets with the title: 'A Sonet of a Louer in praise of his lady./To Calen o Custure me: sung at euerie lines end.' These words belong to the Elizabethan era and were penned, no doubt, by that ubiquitous and prolific gentleman Mr Anon. The original old Gaelic melody, as well as the rest of the words except the Gaelic refrain, are now lost to us. Incidentally, the air found in *William Ballet's Lute Book* is the earliest known annotation of an Irish song and is a variant of that to which 'The Croppy Boy' (the 'Good men and true' version) is sung.

The Spinning Wheel

Mellow the moonlight to shine is beginning,
Close by the window, young Eileen is spinning;
Bent o'er the fire her blind grandmother sitting,
Is crooning and moaning and drowsily knitting.

CHORUS   Merrily, cheerily, noisily whirring
              Spins the wheel, swings the wheel
              While the foot's stirring;
              Sprightly and lightly and airily ringing,
              Sounds the sweet voice of the young maiden singing.

'Eily, *a chara*, I hear someone tapping.'
''Tis the ivy dear granny against the glass flapping.'
'Eily, I surely hear somebody sighing.'
''Tis the sound, mother dear, of the autumn winds dying.'

CHORUS

There's a form at the casement, the form of her true love,
And he whispers with face bent, 'I'm waiting for you love.
Get up on the stool, through the lattice step lightly,
And we'll rove in the grove while the moon's shining brightly.'

CHORUS

Slower and slower and slower the wheel swings.
Lower and lower and lower the reel rings.
E'er the wheel and the reel stop their spinning and moving
Thro' the grove the young lovers by moonlight are roving.

'The Spinning Wheel' is a traditional tune set to words by Francis Waller (1809–1894), a former editor of the *Dublin University Magazine* and contributor to the *Imperial Dictionary of Universal Biography*. It was first published in *Songs Of Irish Wit and Humour* (1884) by A. P. Graves. Delia Murphy, who learnt the song from the well-known priest, Father O'Flynn, made it popular in Ireland.

'The Spinning Wheel' was on the first test recording I made for Decca in London in my late teens. It's a very widely-known song now and it is frequently requested at concerts.

Eibhlin A Rún

Do chaith mé mo bhróga leat, Eibhlin a rún.
Do chaith mé mo bhróga leat, Eibhlin a rún.
Do chaith mé mo bhróga leat,
Do ghearr síos na scórthai leat,
Mar shúil 'sgo mbeinn pósta leat, Eibhlin a rún.

'A' dtiocfaidh tú nó a bhfanóidh tú, Eibhlin a rún?
A' dtiocfaidh tú nó a bhfanóidh tú, Eibhlin a rún?'
'Tiocfai mé 'sní fhanói mé,
Bi romham agus leanfad thú.'
O grá lem' chroi fé rún is tú, Eibhlin a rún.

Céad míle fáilte romhat, Eibhlin a rún
Céad míle fáilte romhat, Eibhlin a rún
Céad míle fáilte romhat
Fáilte 'gus fiche romhat,
O naoi gcéad míle fáilte romhat, Eibhlin a rún.

Eileen My Darling

I wore out my shoes after you, Eileen, my darling.
I wore out my shoes after you, Eileen, my darling.
I wore out my shoes after you
Wore their soles away after you
In the hope of being married to you,
Eileen my darling.

'Will you come with me or will you remain behind,
Will you come with me or will you remain behind,
Eileen my darling?'
'I'll come and I'll not remain behind,
Go before me and I'll follow you.'
O, you are the secret of my heart
Eileen my darling.

A hundred thousand welcomes to you, Eileen, my darling
A hundred thousand welcomes to you, Eileen, my darling
A hundred thousand welcomes to you
A welcome and twenty to you,
Nine hundred thousand welcomes to you
Eileen my darling.

Connemara, one of my favourite areas in Ireland.

Galway Bay viewed from the Connemara shore. Tradition claims that the Eileen of the song was a Connemara girl and if so she would have often seen this or some similar sight.

It is thought that the words of '*Eibhlín A Rún*' were composed by Cearbhall Ó'Dálaigh, a poet and harper from County Carlow who flourished around 1600. It is not certain who composed the music, but, considering Ó'Dálaigh's stature as a poet and musician, it is unlikely that he would have been happy with anything less than original music to accompany such a personal statement of his love for Eibhlín.

The story goes that Eibhlín was from Connemara, the rugged mountainy area to the north of Galway Bay, and that she was engaged to Cearbhall. However, her parents were far from enthusiastic about the match and, when the poet was far away, possibly back home in Carlow, Eibhlín's parents arranged for her to marry someone else. Eventually, when news of Eibhlín's engagement reached Cearbhall, he hurried across country on foot (wearing out the soles of his shoes in the process) and arrived in the nick of time, just as the wedding ceremony was about to begin. The distraught poet then sang his verses at the door of the hall of festivities, asking his beloved to elope with him – which she immediately did!

Believe Me,
if all those Endearing Young Charms

Believe me, if all those endearing young charms
Which I gaze on so fondly today,
Were to change by tomorrow, and fleet in my arms
Like fairy-gifts fading away,
Thou wouldst still be ador'd, as this moment thou art,
Let thy loveliness fade as it will,
And around the dear ruin each wish of my heart
Would entwine itself verdantly still.

It is not while beauty and youth are thine own,
And thy cheeks unprofan'd by a tear,
That the fervour and faith of a soul can be known,
To which time will but make thee more dear:
No, the heart that has truly lov'd never forgets
But as truly loves on to the close,
As the sunflower turns on her god, when he sets,
The same look which she turn'd when he rose.

William Chappell in his huge and influential survey of the songs and music of the British Isles, *Popular Music of the Olden Time* (1855–1859), called the melody of this song 'English', so Sir Charles Stanford and Messrs A. P. Graves (father of poet Robert Graves) and Alfred Moffat omitted the song from their Irish anthologies, even though the words are by Thomas Moore, who did so much for the Irish vocal tradition.

Traditional melodies tend to appear all over the place in 'variants' – some more readily recognisable than others. The tune of 'Believe Me' was first identified as '*Happy Dick Dawson*', which was collected in Limerick in 1740 and, as such, wedded to a set of words, 'I Lo'ed Na a Laddie But Ane', and published in the *Scots Musical Museum* in 1790 – a full fifty years before Bunting published the version which Moore used.

Danny Boy

O Danny Boy! the pipes, the pipes are calling,
From glen to glen and down the mountain side.
The Summer's gone and all the flowers are dying,
'Tis you, 'tis you must go and I must bide.
But come you back when Summer's in the meadow,
Or when the valley's hushed and white with snow,
'Tis I'll be there in sunshine or in shadow,
O Danny Boy! O Danny Boy! I love you so.

And if you come when all the flowers are dying,
And I am dead as dead I well may be,
You'll come and find the place where I am lying,
And kneel and say an Ave there for me.
And I shall hear, though soft you tread above me,
And all my dreams will warmer, sweeter be,
If you will bend and tell me that you love me,
Then I shall sleep in peace until you come to me.

This is the Irish song that people the world over seem to know and want to hear at concerts. It has a special significance for me for a very personal reason. About ten years after I had given up singing for ever, as I thought, I happened to chance upon *Songs of Erin*, the first long-playing album I ever recorded. I asked and received permission to listen to it and, while the record was playing the 'Danny Boy' track, I was moved to tears. I was overcome by the bitter-sweet memory of the circumstances in which the recording had been made, three weeks after my marriage, with my husband by my side in the studio. Though I did not know it (or even want it) at the time, I was on the verge of taking up singing again as a profession. When I hear that verson of 'Danny Boy' now, though the intense emotion is not repeated, my mind harks back to that traumatic moment in the monastic seclusion of Stanbrook Abbey in England.

Ironically, the words of Ireland's most famous song were written by an Englishman, Fred Weatherly, an opera librettist (his text for *Pagliacci* is still the standard English version) who eked out a more lucrative existence writing doggerel for Christmas cards. The tune has attracted countless literary efforts, among them a text by the tenor John McCormack, *O Mary Dear*. But Weatherly was a skilled songwriter whose clever Italianate placing of open vowels on high notes gave his words an immediate appeal. It is worth noticing how he contradicts musical theory by placing the word 'bend' on the highest note in the song. Anyone else would have put it on a low note, and thereby lost the dramatic impact that Weatherly achieved.

Sir Hubert Parry pronounced it to be the most beautiful folk tune in the world. Froud and Lee in their book on *Faeries* claimed that the faeries composed the melody. And why not ...? It was first noted by Jane Ross in Limavady and published as a tune without a title by Petrie in 1855. In Dublin for the first ever performance of *Messiah* in 1742, Handel is supposed to have said that he would willingly sacrifice every note he had written to claim authorship for the tune we now know as 'The Londonderry Air'. If this is so, it took that tune a long time to appear in print.

Ailiú Éanai

Ailiú éanai! ailiú éarai!
Shiúlas an drúcht 's an ghrian ag éirí,
Ailiú éanai! ailiú éarai!
Ailiú éanai! ailiú éarai!
Sheólas mo bhó sa ghleanntán sléibhe,
Ailiú éanai! ailiú éarai!

Ailiú éanai! ailiú éarai!
Fuaireas rómham an táiliúir aerach,
Ailiú éanai! ailiú éarai!

Ailiú éanai! ailiú éarai!
Ag fuagháil cótamór de'n bhréidín,
Ailiú éanai! ailiú éarai!

Ailiú éanai! ailiú éarai!
Nach álainn é mo tháiliúir aerach,
Ailiú éanai! ailiú éarai!

'*Ailiú éanai, ailiú earai*', are yodelling-like calls echoing across the hills. The translation of the middle lines in each verse is as follows:

> I walked in the dew when the sun was rising,
> I drove my cow through the mountain valley,
> I met there the merry tailor,
> Sewing an overcoat made of tweed.
> Isn't my merry tailor a lovely man?

Of all the recordings I've ever made, if I were asked which one I like best, it would be this song sung as it is on Ciarán Mac Mathúna's Gael-linn album, *Mo Cheól Thú*.

Carraig Donn

On Carraig Donn, the heath is brown,
The clouds are dark over Árd na Laoi,
And many a stream comes rushing down
To swell the angry Abha na Bui.
The moaning blast is sweeping fast
Through many a leafless tree,
But I'm alone, for he is gone,
My hawk has flown, *ochón, mo chroi*.

The heath was green on Carraig Donn
Bright shone the sun on Árd na Laoi
The dark green trees bent trembling down,
To kiss the slumbering Abha na Bui.
That happy day, 'twas but last May,
'Tis like a dream to me,
When Dónal swore, aye o'er and o'er,
We'd part no more, a *stór mo chroí*.

Soft April showers and bright May flowers,
Will bring the summer back again,
But will they bring those happier hours,
I spent with my brave Dónal then?
'Tis but a chance, for he's gone to France,
To wear the Fleur-de-Lis
But I'll follow you my Dónal Dubh,
For still I'm true to you, *mo chroí*.

*'But I'm alone, for he is gone
My hawk has flown ochon, mo chroi'*

I first sang this song as the soprano part of a trio with Deirdre Kelleher (nee Flynn) and Kathleen Byrne (nee Watkins) at Sion Hill School in Dublin. The three of us were soon introduced to the celtic harp as an accompanying instrument. About this time (mid fifties), the Irish Tourist Board was promoting *An Tóstal*, a *Festival of Welcome* to attract visitors to Ireland. Much of the publicity was centred in London and, perhaps because the harp has such symbolic significance in Ireland, the three of us schoolgirls were brought to London to help advertise the festival. I then had my first experience of the problems of keeping three harps in tune with each other for any length of time. I fear that there was often a discrepancy of pitch between the harps. We were rushed from one engagement to the next – radio, TV and press – with insufficient time to tune up properly. Deirdre and Kathleen still live in Dublin and we keep in touch.

The song itself 'Carraig Donn' is by Denny Lane, a mid-nineteenth century poet from Cork who contributed regularly to *The Nation*, the official publication of the political movement, 'Young Ireland', which is discussed at greater length in the next chapter. Also discussed in the next chapter are the Wild Geese, those soldiers of fortune who followed Patrick Sarsfield into exile in France after the Williamite war of 1691.

The Dónal Dubh of this song was one of those Wild Geese who had 'gone to France to wear the Fleur-de-Lis'. Carraig Donn may still be recognised in Percy French's 'Mountains of Mourne' but the tune had enjoyed an earlier popularity as that used by Thomas Moore for his Lalla Rookh verse, 'Bendemere's Stream'. The Laoi mentioned in the song is probably the River Lee on which the beautiful city of Cork is built.

I have been to Cork many times giving concerts and, oddly enough, 'Carraig Donn' is not the song that I associate with the city but instead, 'The Bells of Shandon', which my brother Dermot used to sing when I was a child. How could I forget those words which were interminably warbled in every room of our house in Sligo?

> With deep affection and recollection
> I often think of those Shandon bells
> Whose sounds so wild would
> In days of childhood
> Cast round my cradle
> Their magic spells.
> On this I ponder
> Where e'er I wander
> And thus grow fonder
> Sweet Cork of thee.
> But the bells of Shandon
> Sound far more grand on
> The pleasant waters of the River Lee.

From the top of the tower of Shandon church there is a fine panoramic view of Cork city and its environs, but it is the famous 'Bells of Shandon' that attract most visitors to this spot. The church was built in 1722 to replace an older church destroyed in the siege of 1690. The eight bells were cast by Abel Rudhall of Gloucester.

Nine-year-old Dermot sang this song with the local Christian Brothers School Choir in that year's Feis (Festival of Music). Perhaps the endless rehearsing put me off ever singing the song myself, but I do like it and maybe one of these days . . .

I Know Where I'm Going

1. I know where I'm going,
    And I know who's going with me;
    I know who I love,
    But the dear knows who I'll marry!

2. I have stockings of silk,
    Shoes of fine green leather,
    Combs to buckle my hair,
    And a ring for every finger.

3. Some say he's black,
    But I say he's bonny;
    The fairest of them all,
    My handsome winsome Johnny.

4. Feather beds are soft,
    And painted rooms are bonny;
    But I would leave them all,
    To go with my love Johnny.

5. I know where I'm going,
    And I know who's going with me,
    I know who I love,
    But the dear knows who I'll marry.

'I Know Where I'm Going' is another song from the Herbert Hughes collection. He learnt it from his nurse Ellen Boylan who came to the Hughes household in Belfast from the Sperrin Mountains when she was sixteen years old. For Hughes, she was a rich storehouse of traditional music and most of the songs in his first volume of *Irish Country Songs* (1909) came from her. 'I Know Where I'm Going' is a fragment of something which was evidently longer and many of the phrases recur in other songs in various parts of the English-speaking world.

Úna Bhán

A Úna bhán, a bhlá na ndlaoi ómhrach,
Tar éis do bháis de bharr droch chomhairle,
Feach, a ghrá ci'ca b'fhearr de'n dá chomhairle.
A éin i gcliabhán, is mé in Átha na Donoige.

A Úna bhán ba rós i ngáirdín thú,
's ba choinnléoir óir ar bhord na banrioghna
*   thú;*
Ba cheileabhar 's ba cheólmhar ag gabhail an
*   bhealaigh seo rómham thú,*
'S é mo chreach maidne brónach nár pósadh
*   liom thú.*

A Úna bhán, 's tú do mhearaigh mo chiall,
A Úna is tú a chuaidh go dlú idir mé 's Dia;
A Úna an chraoibh chumhra, a lúibín casta na
*   gciabh,*
Nár bhfear dhomhsa bheith gan súile ná
*   d'fheiceáil 'riamh.*

Fair Úna

Fair Úna, flower of the golden locks,
You have died as a result of bad advice.
Look, my love, which advice was better?
A bird in a cage and I waiting at Átha na
    Donóige.

Fair Úna, you were as a rose in a garden;
A golden candlestick on the queen's table,
Moving before me like a song.
'Tis my black sorrow that you were not
    married to me.

Fair Úna, 'tis you who has bereft me of
    my senses;
Úna, 'tis you who've come between me
    and God.
Oh Úna of the scented blossom, of the
    ringleted wavy hair,
It were better for me if I had been blind
    and never to have set eyes on you.

Here is one of Ireland's finest Gaelic love songs in the true classic folk tradition. It is only in the past couple of decades or so that songs like this, from the rich musical heritage of Gaelic-speaking Ireland, have come to be appreciated to any extent outside our own country. While some people were aware of the existence of folk melodies similar to those found in other countries, very few knew about, or even knew of, the music of the highly-skilled composers who carried on their work in the finest traditions of the bards. Many of their songs, among then 'Úna Bhán', have achieved such perfection of artistic expression that they have rightly been ranked with the greatest *chansons* and *liede*. The *amhrán mór* or 'high song' of Gaelic Ireland is, in my opinion, unsurpassed, not only in its emotional range, but also in its structure. These songs are superb examples of the union of fine poetry and inspired music; it is because of the great demands that this art makes on a performer that it has so few exponents.

The hero of 'Úna Bhán' is Tomás Láidir Mac Coisteala, who had fallen in love with Úna the daughter of one McDermot, the owner of Castle Carrick on an island in Lough Key, County Roscommon. The story goes that McDermot confined his daughter to the castle on the island and forbade her to marry or even see her love. Mac Coisteala had made plans to elope with Úna and waded his horse back and forth to the island waiting for a signal from her, but none ever came. Eventually news reached the poet that Úna had died. After her death his grief knew no bounds, and he regularly swam his horse to the island to visit her grave where, one morning, he too was found dead.

Seán Óg Ó'Tuama, my great friend and mentor, introduced me to this song when I returned to Dublin, a widow after fifteen months of marriage. Seán Óg, one of the busiest people I have ever known, was generous to a fault where his friends were concerned. My debt to him is enormous. I had only to send him a postcard or phone him saying I'd be in Dublin and would like to see him about some songs, and he would drop everything and meet me at the appointed place. Over a meal he would teach me songs from his vast reservoir of Celtic music. Painstakingly, we would go over the song together, word for word, until I got the accent and intonation as perfectly as I could manage. Often he had no time to write out the music in advance or bring proper manuscript paper with him and, on those occasions, he used whatever was most readily available. I still have a song written by him on a paper napkin and another on a flattened out sick bag I had brought with me from the plane. Father O'Flynn, who taught Delia Murphy 'The Spinning Wheel', was Seán Óg's great teacher and inspiration in his work reviving old Gaelic songs.

Lough Key, the location for 'Úna Bhán', is within an hour's drive of my childhood home in Sligo. Not far away from the lough on the banks of the River Boyle stand the silent ruins of the Cistercian Abbey of Boyle, founded by Abbot Maurice O'Duffy in 1161. I lingered there for a while one fresh April morning when I was visiting Lough Key, finding the quietness and the pastoral scene conducive to prayer, before making my way to the site of Úna Bhán's tragedy.

OPPOSITE *Lough Key, County Roscommon. In the background is the castle where fair Una was imprisoned and eventually died, probably of a broken heart. The day I visited the place was wintry though bright and shiney. A vast national park surrounds the lake which is also a meeting place for the scores of boats that traverse the lakes and rivers of the area.*

She Lived Beside the Anner

She lived beside the Anner
At the foot of Slievenamon,
A gentle peasant girl with mild eyes like the dawn.
Her lips were dewy rose buds, her teeth of pearls rare,
And a snowdrift 'neath a beechen bough,
Her neck and nut-brown hair.
How pleasant was to meet her on Sunday, when the bell
Was filling with mellow tones lone wood and grassy dell.
And when at eve young maidens strayed the river bank along,
The widow's brown-haired daughter was loveliest of the throng.
Ah, cold and well nigh callous this weary heart has grown,
For thy helpless fate dear Ireland and for sorrows of my own.
Yet a tear my eye will moisten when by Anner-side I stray,
For the lily of the mountain-foot that withered far away.

The words of 'She Lived Beside the Anner' are by Charles Joseph Kickham (1828–1882), a Young Irelander who joined the Fenian Movement in 1860. Poet, novelist and short-story writer, his best work is thought to be the novel *Knock-nagow*. The tune for 'She Lived Beside the Anner' is traditional.

The River Anner runs into the River Suir ('Calen O Custure Me') not far from the historic town of Clonmel in County Tipperary. Other songs like '*Sliabh na mBan*', '*Dia Luain Dia Mairt*' and '*The Fairy Tree*' originate in this traditionally cultured area of Ireland. In my younger and less informed days, I used to think that the well-known song 'It's A Long Way To Tipperary' came from there too and I was surprised to discover that 'Tipperary' was the nickname Irish soldiers in the British army had for Soho, London's notorious red-light district – much like 'The Holy Ground' in another famous song which was a euphemism used by sailors for a similar area in Cobh, a County Cork port.

Bring Me a Shawl From Galway

1. Bring me a shawl from Galway,
      a purple shawl from Galway;
    'T would only show the love I know,
      for Christie in a small way.
    May day, my day, it will be ages
      till Friday;
    All Aranmore and Inishmaan will
      tar their curraghs and come along,
    With the sea breeze helping our
        summer song
      and the blue skies shining on my
        day.

2. Bring me a shawl from Galway;
    Bring creamy lace from Galway,
    Where moonlight beams o'er crystal
        streams
      thro' every day and all day.
    May day, my day, sailing the waters
      on Friday.
    All Aranmore and Inishmaan will
      tar their curraghs and come along
    With the sea breeze helping our
        summer song
      and the blue skies beaming on my
        day.
    Bring me a silken snow white
        neckerchief like the moonlight
    And creamy lace like dazzling foam
        upon the rocks in sunlight.

3. All you could bring from Galway,
    Bright ocean pearls from Galway
    Could not compare with the love I
        bear
      for Christie ever and alway.
    Galway, Galway, bring Christie Ryan
        from Galway,
      I want him here in Inishere
      For every day and all day.
    Ah sure no one knows but widow
        Rose,
      The longing I have for my day.

I first heard this song sung by the late Charles Kennedy when I took part in an Irish Heritage concert in London some years ago. I liked it at once, not least because of the attraction Galway and the Aran Islands have always had for me.

When I was a teenager in the fifties, it was the 'in thing' for those involved with anything Gaelic, or even literary, in the circles I moved in to visit the Gaelic-speaking Aran Islands.

The three islands, Inishmore, Inishmaan and Inishere, guard the entrance to Galway Bay. They have acquired a certain mystique, partly due to Robert Flaherty's classic film, *Man of Aran*, and partly to the writings of people like John Millington Synge who lived on Inishmaan for a while and wrote *Riders to the Sea* and *The Playboy of the Western World*, based on his contact with the island. Other writers native to the islands, like Liam O'Flaherty, Tom O'Flaherty and, more recently, Brendán Ó'Éithir, have kept the mystique alive.

When I first met Richard Selig, the young American poet, he was on his way to the Aran Islands. He loved the island people and their way of life, as I do myself, and it was from Inishere that he sent the longest and most interesting letter he ever wrote to me, part of which is reproduced on p. 178. It was there also that he composed the first section of his long poem 'The Coast'.

Later, when we got married, we spent our honeymoon on Inishere. We travelled to the island in a sailing boat which was carrying turf from Carraroe on the Connemara coast. These sailing boats, known as Connemara hookers, brought turf to fuel fires on the islands for centuries but, now that the trade in turf is no more, the hookers too have disappeared. Because there is no pier on Inishere, we were met about a quarter of a mile off shore by a canvas- and tar-covered curragh and rowed to the beach. These are the curraghs of the song.

Nowadays, the islands are more accessible and have their own air service to the mainland. I flew Aer Arann when I visited Inishmore for the first time in the spring of 1976. I stayed with my friends the O'Toole family in Bungowla, on the

---

The curragh is a seafaring vessel peculiar to the west coast of Ireland. It is constructed of tarred canvas stretched over a wooden frame and in the skilled hands of the Aranmen it virtually dances on top of the Atlantic waves. It is light enough to be pulled up on the strand and carried on the shoulders of two men over the rocks away from the sea

ABOVE AND LEFT *It was at Sean O'Congaile's guest-house in Inishere that I stayed during my honeymoon on the Aran Islands. At that time donkey and cart was the sole mode of transport on the island. Curraghs ferried passengers and cargo from boat to beach, and donkeys or shanks mare brought things the rest of the way. There is still no motor-car on Inishere though the airstrip at the edge of the beach ensures that the visitor reaches the outside world more quickly.*

west side of the island and gave a concert of Gaelic songs in the parish hall at Kilronan, the island's capital and main harbour. The island is dotted with ancient monastic ruins, which interest me very much, and also with intriguing prehistoric stone forts which have baffled archaeologists for centuries.

Dún Aengus is the most famous fort of its type in western Europe. I visited it with a friend, walking there along miles of 300-foot-high cliffs, sheer precipices with seagulls and cormorants nestling on the ledges below, which reminded us of some of Liam O'Flaherty's nature stories. Most intriguing of all for me were the stone walls set like lace-work against the sky. These walls are constructed, not with the rounded boulders one finds along the seashore, but with jagged stones that hang together in a manner that seems to defy the laws of gravity, if

not of nature itself, and manage year after year to withstand the fierce relentless Atlantic gales that hit the islands in winter.

Galway city, the Aran people's gateway to the outside world, holds many memories for me, among them holidays there as a child and another delightful spell on my own in Gaelic-speaking Spiddal to the west of the city. According to *The Annals of the Four Masters*, a fort was erected at Galway in 1124 by the Connachtmen. *The Annals of the Four Masters* is one of the most important sources of early Irish church history and genealogy, compiled in the seventeenth century by four friars from the Franciscan friary near Donegal town. In 1232, when Richard de Burgh took the city and made it his residence, Galway became a flourishing Anglo-Norman colony and, among its settlers, were the families who were later known as the Fourteen Tribes of Galway: the Blakes, Bodkins,

Brownes, D'Arcys, ffrenches, Kirwins, Joyces, Lynches, Morrisses, Martins, Skerrets, Athys, Deans and fforts.

There is a story that one mayor Lynch of Galway went against the advice of his council and hanged his own son for murder, thus giving the English language a new word. For a long time the settlers looked with disfavour, to say the least, at the native Irish who inhabited the surrounding countryside and a by-law of 1518 decreed 'that neither O nor Mac shall strutte ne swagger thro' the streets of Galway'. This did not deter the native Irish from making the odd foray into the city as an inscription on the west gate of the town at one time seemed to suggest: 'From the fury of the O'Flahertys, good Lord deliver us.' The O'Flahertys were Connemara people. My mother, Mai Kirwin, was a Galway woman and a descendant of one of the Tribes. It was as undergraduates at the university at Galway that my parents first met.

The words of 'Bring Me a Shawl From Galway' were written by Crawford Neil, a young Irish poet, who was a contemporary of W. B. Yeats. Like Yeats and others of this period of Celtic twilight, he was involved with the Irish literary revival which explains his fascination with the Aran Islands. He died in his early twenties, shot by accident while sightseeing in Dublin during the uprising of 1916. The words of the song are sung to music by Joseph Crofts.

The Cross of Moone is an 8th century celtic cross depicting the Adam and Eve story, the sacrifice of Isaac and Daniel in the lion's den. High crosses, sometimes referred to as celtic crosses, are Europe's finest stone carvings in the first milleneum after Christ. The term 'High Cross' was used as far back as 957 and one hundred and fifty of them survive today, in whole or in part, throughout Ireland. Those found in Leinster and Ulster belong to the 8th century and those in Connacht were carved in the 12th century. The carvings on the crosses illustrate chiefly biblical events and were probably intended as 'picture bibles' used in the instruction of the illiterate public as much as the continental frescoes were used – (the Irish churches were too small and dark for frescoes). Some scholars hold that the carvings were also painted in many different colours. It is believed that originally, these stone crosses stood at focal points probably beside the church – inside monastic enclosures.

Padraig the Fiddler

1. Padraig sits in the garden,
    In undher the bright new moon,
    An' from his fiddle he coaxes,
    A lovely dreamy tune.

2. Och! I love the tune he's playing,
    And wisht it was for me,
    But I know its for the birdeens
    'Way up in the cherry tree.

3. Sure every night they peep from
    In undher their mother's wings,
    Tae hear the silvery music
    His wee dark fiddle sings.

4. An' for them he's always playing,
    An' has nae a thought for me;
    For if I go out he wandhers
    Away from the cherry tree.

When I was seventeen I sang this song at the *Feis Ceóil* in Dublin and felt privileged to be accompanied on the piano by no less a person than Jenny Redden, who was regarded as Ireland's accompanist par excellence. She is Ireland's equivalent to England's Gerald Moore. The words of the song are by Padraic Gregory and the music by John F. Larchet.

Ar Éirinn Ní n-Eósainn Ce h-Í

For Ireland I'd Not Tell Her Name

Aréir is mé téarnamh um' neóin,
Ar an dtaobh thall den teóra 'na mbím,
Do théarnaig an spéir-bhean am' chómair
D'fhág taomanach breóite lag sinn.
Do ghéilleas dá méin is dá cló,
Dà béal tanaí beó mhilis binn,
Do léimeas fé dhéin dul 'na cómhair,
Is ar Éirinn ní n-eosainn cé h-í.

Dá ngéilleadh an spéir-bhean dom ghlór,
Siad ráidhte mo bheól a bheadh fíor;
Go deimhin duit go ndéanfainn a gnó
Do léirchur i gcóir is i gcrich.
Do léighfinn go léir stair dom' stór,
'Sba mhéinn liom í thógaint dom chroi.
'S Do bhéarfainn an chraobh dhi ina dóid,
Is ar Éirinn ní n-eosainn ce h-í.

Tá spéir -bhruinneal mhaordha dheas óg,
Ar an taobh thall de'n teóra 'na mbím.
Tá féile 'gus daonnacht is meóin
Is deise ró mhór ins an mhnaoi,
Tá folt lei a' tuitim go feóir,
Go cocanach ómarach buí.
Tá lasadh 'na leacain mar rós,
Is ar Éirinn Ní n-Eosainn cé hí.

Last night as I strolled abroad
On the far side of my farm
I was approached by a comely maiden
Who left me distraught and weak.
I was captivated by her demeanour and shapeliness
By her sensitive and delicate mouth
I hastened to approach her
But for Ireland I'd not tell her name.

If only this maiden heeded my words,
What I'd tell her would be true.
Indeed I'd devote myself to her
And see to her welfare.
I would regale her with my story
And I longed to take her to my heart
Where I'd grant her pride of place
But for Ireland I'd not tell her name.

There is a beautiful young maiden
On the far side of my farm.
Generosity and kindness shine in her face
With the exceeding beauty of her countenance.
Her hair reaches to the ground
Sparkling like yellow gold;
Her cheeks blush like the rose
But for Ireland I'd not tell her name.

The melody of this song (like that of 'Calen O Custure Me') has travelled far. Clondillon relates hearing a Roumanian folk singer sing the tune believing it to be a Roumanian folksong. Perhaps some soldier of fortune belonging to the Wild Geese had the gift of song!

Seán Óg explained the story to me like this: a young man fell secretly in love with a girl. Too poor to support her and too shy to propose, he went abroad to seek his fortune. However, when he returned to claim his beloved, he was shattered to find her married to his brother. Still in love, he composed this song to her but, for obvious reasons, refused to reveal her name.

The Song of Glendun

In Glendun, County Antrim, reflecting on the words of the song.

Sure this is blessed Érin an' this the same glen,
The gold is on the whinbush, the water sings again,
The fairy thorn's in flower, an' what ails my heart then?
Flower o' the May, flower o' the May,
What about the May-time an' he far away!

Summer loves the green glen, the white bird loves the sea,
An' the wind must kiss the heather top, an' the red bell hides a bee;
As the bee is dear to the honey flower, so one is dear to me.
Flower o' the rose, flower o' the rose,
A thorn pricked me one day, but nobody knows.

The bracken up the brae-side has rusted in the air,
Three birches lean together, so silver limbed and fair;
Och! golden leaves are flyin' fast, but the scarlet roan is rare.
Berry o' the roan, berry o' the roan,
The wind sighs among the trees, but I sigh alone.

I knit beside the turf fire, and spin upon the wheel,
Winter nights for thinking long, round runs the wheel.
But he never knew, he never knew, that here for him I'd kneel.
Sparkle o' the fire, sparkle o' the fire,
Mother Mary, keep my love, an' send me my desire.

I first heard 'The Song of Glendun' when I was a child competing at the annual *Feis* in Sligo. The words are taken from Moira O'Neill's *Songs of the Glens of Antrim* with music by Carl G. Hardebeck. I had forgotten all about 'The Song of Glendun' until recently, when a friend played a beautiful recording of it by Bernadette Greevy. I've since sung it as an example of an Irish art song on a BBC Radio 3 programme. I think it is as hauntingly beautiful as the famous nine Glens of Antrim which open on to the sea along the picturesque coastline north of Larne, the gateway to the glens.

Not long ago, while I was in Belfast recording a UTV programme, I took the opportunity to travel north to see for myself the splendour of Glendun, so highly praised in the song. The coastal area through which I drove must be one of the most beautiful in Ireland. The winding road which runs close to the water's edge allowed me to enjoy one magnificent view after another, each new sight of sea, bay and headland affording fresh delight.

I never tire of looking at cromlechs, dolmens and other ancient stones especially after seeing Bob Quinn's exquisite film *Cloch* (meaning stone) on BBC television in 1981. Such was the power and beauty of this film that I was more profoundly moved by it than by any television programme I've seen before or since. So it was a particular treat to come across the group of standing stones called Ossian's Grave on the slopes of Tievebulliagh near the town of Cushendall some miles south of Glendun.

ABOVE *Newgrange in the Boyne valley, County Meath, the most sophisticated of all Irish megalithic tombs dating from 2,500 BC.*

OPPOSITE *The Carrowmore Dolmen, County Sligo. Dolmens mark ancient burial sites. They generally consist of one or more capstones, supported by a number of boulders or slabs. Here at Carrowmore is the largest group of megalithic remains in the British Isles. It was on this lonely stretch of road that fairies were alleged to have tried to pull my grandfather off his bicycle. In the background is the grave of the mythological Queen Maeve buried on top of Knocknarea (Hill of the Kings).*

The Lark in the Clear Air

Dear thoughts are in my mind
And my soul soars enchanted,
As I hear the sweet lark sing
In the clear air of the day.
For a tender beaming smile
To my hope has been granted,
And tomorrow she shall hear
All my fond heart would say.

I shall tell her all my love,
All my soul's adoration,
And I think she will hear
And will not say me nay.
It is this that gives my soul
All its joyous elation,
As I hear the sweet lark sing
In the clear air of the day.

'The Lark in the Clear Air' is a tender love song and a very popular one. Recorded by Sydney MacEwan in 1932, the words were written by Sir Samuel Ferguson of Belfast in about 1850 and set to a traditional melody known as *'Caisleán U, Néill'*, which was collected in the west of Ireland by Lady Ferguson.

My Brown-haired Boy

1. My true love, he dwells in the mountain,
    Like a war-eagle fearless and free;
    By the side of the low tuning fountain,
    That wander thro' sweet Analee.
    For his heart has more truth and more honour,
    Than a king with his palace and crown,
    For the blood of the race of O'Connor,
    Fills the veins of my *Buachaillín Donn*.

2. Soft *céad míle fáilte* I give him,
    When he comes every Sunday to me;
    And what can I do but believe him,
    As he whispers '*a chuisle mo chroí*'.
    For the look is so truthful and tender,
    In his wide roving eyes of dark brown,
    That I'm sure e'en a lady of splendour
    Would be coaxed by my *Buachaillín Donn*.

3. My father has riches in plenty,
    And suitors for me in his eye,
    But oh! let my age come to twenty,
    Ah then, I'll give them all the goodbye.
    For I sigh for a life on the mountain,
    Far away from the dust of the town,
    With the song of the low tuning fountain,
    And the love of my *Buachaillín Donn*.

This brings us to the end of a selection of songs dealing mainly with love between man and woman. The next section deals with another type of love song: the love that a person has for his or her country – in this case Ireland. 'Dark Rosaleen' is a translation of '*Róisín Dubh*', the poetic name for Ireland during a particularly bleak period of the country's history.

The Scent of the Roses

1. Farewell! but whenever you welcome the hour
    That awakens the night-song of mirth in your bower,
    Then think of the friend who once welcom'd it too,
    And forgot his own grief to be happy with you.
    His griefs may return, not a hope may remain
    Of the few that have brighten'd his pathway of pain,
    But he ne'er will forget the short vision that threw
    Its enchantment around him, while ling'ring with you.

2. And still on that evening when pleasure fills up
    To the highest top-sparkle each heart and each cup,
    Where 'er my path lies, be it gloomy or bright,
    My soul, happy friends, will be with you that night;
    Shall join in your revels, your sports, and your wiles,
    And return to me, beaming all o'er with your smiles –
    Too blest, if it tells me that, 'mid the gay cheer
    Some kind voice had murmur'd, 'I wish he were here!'

3. Let Fate do her worst, there are relics of joy,
    Bright dreams of the past, which she cannot destroy;
    Which come in the night-time of sorrow and care,
    And bring back the features that joy used to wear.
    Long, long be my heart with such memories fill'd!
    Like the vase, in which roses have once been distill'd –
    You may break, you may shatter the vase, if you will,
    But the scent of the roses will hang round it still.

'The Scent of the Roses' has been in my repertoire from my earliest singing days when I first began playing the harp at Sion Hill School in Dublin. It is one of Thomas Moore's poems set to the traditional melody '*Moll Rúin*'. Very much a period piece, it may be criticised by some, but I've always found the song attractive and I like the last verse so much that I used the phrase 'The scent of the roses' as the title of my autobiography. The old airs on which Thomas Moore based his melodies were authentic folk music and that may be one reason why so many of his songs took root so quickly among the Irish. 'The Scent of the Roses' is a nostalgic recollection of old friends and times gone by, and the tune to which it is set first appeared in Aird's *Selection of Scotch, English, Irish and Foreign Airs*, published in 1788.

Chapter II

Róisín Dubh

A Róisín ná bíodh brón ort ná cás anois.
Tá do phárdún ón Róimh is ón bPápa 'gat.
Tá na bráithre a' teacht thar sáile 's a' triall
    thar muir,
'S ní cealfar fíon Spáinneach ar mo Róisín Dubh.

Tá grá agam 'm lár duit lé bliain anois;
Grá cráite, grá casmhar, grá ciapaithe,
Grá d'fhág mé gan sláinte gan rian gan rith,
'S go bráth, bráth, gan aon fhághail agam ar
    mo Róisín Dubh.

Beidh an fharraige na tuilte dearga 's an spéir
    'na fuil,
Beidh an saol 'na chogadh chraoragh 'gus
    réabfar cnuic,
Beidh gach gleann sléibhe ar fud Éireann 's
    móinte ar crith,
Lá éigin sul a n-éagfaidh mo Róisín Dubh

Dark Rosaleen

O *Róisín* do not be sorrowful,
Your pardon is assured from Rome and
    the Pope;
The brethren are already put to sea
And Spanish wine will not be denied to
    my *Róisín Dubh*.

There is a terrible love in my heart for you
    for a year now,
An aching tortured anguished love,
A love that has deprived me of health and
    rest
And for ever beyond my reach is my
    Róisín Dubh.

The sea will be in crimson flood and the
    sky rain blood;
The world will be ablaze with war and
    mountains torn asunder,
Every mountain glen and bog in Ireland
    will shake
Some day ere you perish, my *Róisín Dubh*.

'*Róisín Dubh*' (literally, 'Little Black Rose') is one of my favourite Gaelic songs. It's a song of great emotion, thought to have been originally a love song, but for the past century it has been treated as a patriotic song, perhaps *the* patriotic song, of the Gael. I have an abiding love for it because of the intensity and passion of the music and the words. There are numerous versions, but the shortened Gaelic one above is the one I sing in concert, having first introduced it to the audience with a brief summary. James Clarence Mangan's translation of '*Róisín Dubh*' is a poem in its own right and from him we obtain the title, 'Dark Rosaleen'.

For those versed in the lore and history of Ireland, the term *Róisín Dubh* is an evocative one that has long been used to personify the country, which explains why 'Dark Rosaleen' can be regarded as one of Ireland's most famous songs. It's a Gaelic art song that belongs to that genre I call classic-folk and was clearly crafted by people still in possession of many of the bardic skills. Other songs in the same genre are '*Sliabh na mBan*' (p. 79) and '*Eibhlin a Rún*'. I believe that it is impossible to do full justice to these songs without a knowledge of the language and of the social and historical background from which the songs arose.

'*Róisín Dubh*' belongs to a depressed (even oppressed) era in Irish history. After the battle of Kinsale (1603) the old Gaelic order in Ireland started to disintegrate. It hardly required the Battle of the Boyne (1690) and the ensuing Williamite conquest of Ireland to deal it a death blow. Gaelic literature was proscribed and went into a decline from which it never recovered.

During this period the poets of the Gaelic tradition stubbornly and unrealistically clung to a vision of a Stuart return to the throne of England and chose to see this as the only hope of national survival for Ireland. These poets, who by now had lost their honoured public status in the community, invented a literary device called *aisling* (vision), in which Ireland, in the guise of a beautiful woman, comes to visit the poet in a dream. The woman foretells the eventual liberation of Ireland by a Stuart. Even after Culloden (1745) when the Stuart cause was effectively dead, the *Aisling* Poets, with both feet firmly but unrealistically planted in the air, continued to compose their *aisling* poems. Reality had lost hold of them and they were obsessed by their own invention, the *aisling*. Help was coming, they claimed, from Spain and from Rome; there would be a great war in Ireland and the people would rise up and Ireland would once more be Gaelic and free.

As a literary device, the *aisling* worked well and the survival in the popular tradition of songs like '*Róisín Dubh*' can be attributed as much to good poetry as to the skill with which the words were wedded to melodies already popular among the people. Because of the period when poets, harpers and musicians of all kinds were officially proscribed in Ireland and regarded by the state as dangerous to public order, patriotic or national songs of a folk character are remarkably scarce in Gaelic, and '*Róisín Dubh*' was raised to that category only in the last century. Mentioning the name of Ireland in song during the early eighteenth century was forbidden and so poets resorted to the use of secret love names for their country.

James Clarence Mangan, on the other hand, believed that '*Róisín Dubh*' belonged to the Elizabethan era and that it referred to Red Hugh O'Donnell, who, with Hugh O'Neill, the Earl of Tyrone, fought Gaelic Ireland's last war against England (1594–1603). Many others, however, see the song as only the allegorical expression of political discontent in Ireland. But, whatever the origin of the song itself, it is unlikely that '*Róisín Dubh*' as a secret name for Ireland remained a secret to state officials for long. They must have turned a blind eye. Spanish wine mentioned in the song refers to military help from Spain who was then Ireland's ally.

'*Róisín Dubh*' is a strong song. It speaks of loyalty and love – true and fierce, yet not without a vein of tenderness. Here, as in so many of the other love songs in the Gaelic tradition, nature has a prominent place. The ancient Gaelic tradition is full of nature poetry and nowhere does it leave its benevolent mark more than on popular folksong.

Jackets Green

When I was a maiden fair and young
On the pleasant banks of Lee,
No bird that in the greenwood sang
Was half so blithe and free.
My heart n'er beat with flying feet,
No love sang me his queen,
Till down the glen rode Sarsfield's men
And they wore their jackets green.

When William stormed with shot and shell
At the walls of Garryowen,
'Twas in the breech my Dónal fell,
And he sleeps 'neath the Treaty Stone.
That breech the foeman never crossed
While he swung his broadsword keen,
But I do not weep my Dónal dead,
For he fell in his jacket green.

'Jackets Green', written by Michael Scanlan (1836–1900), belongs to another era, born of a mentality quite different from that of the tradition which produced *Róisín Dubh*. While the *aisling* poet dreamt of an imaginary Stuart king, the heroes of 'Jackets Green' are Sarsfield's men. Patrick Sarsfield has always had an honoured and undisputed place in the pantheon of Irish patriots. Descended from the O'Moores of Leinster, he was an 'ex-English' nobleman of the Pale and a brigadier in King James' army. In defeat as much as in victory, Sarsfield kept his honour unblemished and it was eventually his unhappy lot to sign the Treaty of Limerick in 1691 which acknowledged King William's victory. Only in defeat was he given command of the army, but his bold enterprises on the field of battle lived on after him in song and story.

After the Treaty of Limerick, he led the Irish Brigade of 11,000 men to fight as mercenaries on the continent of Europe. The Wild Geese, as those Irish soldiers of fortune were called, helped the French win many a victory over the English when they fought, as they often did, for Louis XIV. English law forbade ships to take young Irishmen – potential soldiers or priests – to the continent and so emigrants were smuggled aboard and entered in the logbooks as 'wild geese'. The name stuck. These Wild Geese played an important role in battles such as Fontenoy, Ramilles, Blenheim and Landen – European continental battles that were celebrated in Ireland in song and story for generations.

The war cry of the Irish Brigade was 'Remember Limerick', a reference to the treaty signed in good faith by Sarsfield and King William but later repudiated by the British parliament. The stone on which the treaty was signed can still be seen today marking one end of the Thomond bridge which spans the River Shannon in Limerick city. Patrick Sarsfield, an officer of France, was killed at the battle of Landen and his last words are alleged to have been 'if only it were for Ireland'.

For a long time the feats of Sarsfield and his Wild Geese salvaged the self-respect of the defeated Irish in the years after 1690. 'Jackets Green' was written much later than the period to which it refers and was the product of a new emerging Anglo-Irish tradition. Songs such as this revived, perhaps even created, a nationalistic spirit in the dark days following the Treaty of Limerick. Some argue that modern Irish nationalism started with Dean Swift (born in Dublin in 1667), the beginning of a long line of 'Englishmen in exile' (Frank O'Connor's description), Irish nationalists like Tone, Emmet, Parnell, Pearse and, finally, Childers whose son was to become president of the Irish Republic in the 1970s.

Down by the Glenside

'Twas down by the glenside I met an old woman,
A plucking young nettles, nor saw I was coming.
I listened a while to the song she was humming,
Glory-o, glory-o, to the bold Fenian men.

'Tis fifty long years since I saw the moon beaming
On strong manly forms and on eyes with hope gleaming;
I see them again sure thro' all my day-dreaming,
Glory-o, glory-o, to the bold Fenian men.

I passed on my way, God be praised that I met her;
Be life long or short I will never forget her.
We may have great men, but we'll never have better,
Glory-o, glory-o, to the bold Fenian men.

The eighteenth century dawned upon a defeated Ireland brooding under the dark clouds of the penal laws. The Treaty of Limerick (1691) signed by Patrick Sarsfield and the Representative of King William, was never ratified by the English parliament. For the next century, the Catholic majority in Ireland was relentlessly persecuted. There were frequent rebellions against the English, starting a diabolically vicious cycle of oppression and revolt which continued into the twentieth century. This gave birth to an underground as well as a hidden Ireland. Revolt required little encouragement and the spirit of the French and American Revolutions added fuel, if such were needed, to the fire. There was the United Irishman uprising of 1798 and the Young Ireland uprising of 1848. Irish nationalism, as we know it today, was stirring into life and the writings of one generation affected the actions of the next. The Young Ireland movement looked for inspiration to Ireland's past and preached self-reliance. The movement attracted people of the highest calibre in the Irish society of the day, as the following story illustrates.

In the Young Ireland uprising, nine of the leaders were captured, tried and convicted of treason against Her Majesty, the Queen, and sentenced to death. Before passing sentence, the judge asked if there was anything anyone wished to say. Thomas Meagher, speaking for all, said: 'My lord, this is our first offence but not our last. If you will be easy with us this once, we promise, on our word as gentlemen, to try to do better next time. And next time – sure we won't be fools to get caught.' Immediately the indignant judge sentenced them all to be hanged, drawn and quartered. Passionate protest from all over the world forced Queen Victoria to commute the sentence to transportation for life to a penal colony in Australia.

In 1874 word reached the astounded Queen that the Sir Charles Duffy who had just been elected Prime Minister of Australia was the same Charles Duffy who had been transported twenty-five years previously and, at the Queen's request, the records of the other convicts were checked with the following results:

Thomas Francis Meagher, Governor of Montana.
Terence McManus, Brigadier General, US Army.
Patrick Donahue, Brigadier General, US Army.
Richard O'Gorman, Governor General of Newfoundland.
Morris Lyene, Attorney General of Australia, in which office Michael
    Ireland succeeded him.
Thomas D'Arcy McGee, Member of Parliament, Montreal, Minister of
    Agriculture and President of Council Dominion of Canada.
John Mitchell, prominent New York politician. This man was the father
    of John Purroy Mitchell, Mayor of New York at the outbreak of
    World War I.

Young Ireland was an intellectual as well as a political movement and it promoted research into Ireland's musical and literary past. The Belfast Harp Festival (1792) had brought together the last of the great Irish harpers, the final remnants of a dying breed, and Thomas Moore's *Irish Melodies* (1808–1834) provided sustenance for the Irish spirit by wedding nostalgic words to the almost forgotten Irish airs. Queen Elizabeth I had once ordered Lord Barrymore to silence the harp and 'hang the harpers wherever found' but Young Ireland had made the harp their emblem, and for a motto they adopted the phrase: 'It is new strung and it shall be heard.' In the 1860s, the Fenian movement took over where Young Ireland left off. Named after Fion McCumhaill, one of Ireland's legendary mythological heroes, the Fenian movement fired the popular imagination and inspired many songs in its own day and later. One of those songs is 'Down by the Glenside' written by Peadar Kearney, who also composed '*Amhrán na bhFiann*', Ireland's national anthem.

Irish and Anglo-Saxon illumination. From Macregol Gospels, 9th century.

Ornamented page   *St Mark*

The Minstrel Boy

The Minstrel Boy to the war is gone,
In the ranks of the dead you'll find him;
His father's sword he has girded on,
And his wild harp slung behind him.
'Land of song', said the warrior bard,
'Though all the world betray thee,
One sword, at least, thy rights shall guard,
One faithful harp shall praise thee.'

The Minstrel fell – but the foeman's chain
Could not bring his proud soul under;
The harp he lov'd ne'er spoke again,
For he tore its chords asunder;
And said, 'No chains shall sully thee,
Thou soul of love and bravery.
Thy songs were made for the pure and
         free,
They shall never sound in slavery.'

The melody of 'The Minstrel Boy' is from Edward Bunting's collection and the words are by Thomas Moore. The theme is the ill-fated United Irishman rebellion of 1798 – a rebellion encouraged by Wolfe Tone, the father of Irish Republicanism. By linking together the harp, the minstrel, the sword and rebellion, Thomas Moore forged a nationalistic image, which is still dear to the heart of Irish republicans. The harp is one of the national emblems of Ireland and as such appears on official documents, coins and, incredibly, the bottle of Guinness.

Music was an integral part of Gaelic Ireland's way of life, a fact commented on by Giraldus Cambrensis, chronicler to the Norman invaders of Ireland in 1169. As we have already seen, in an effort to destroy that way of life, the invaders of Elizabethan times proscribed musicians and their music. It became common official practice to burn harps wherever they were found. During the Cromwellian era, harpers were required to carry identity cards in the form of government permits.

However, it is only fair to say that traditional and/or bardic musicians in England were also forbidden by law for a period after Queen Elizabeth I's reign. Ballad singers were outlawed by the state and looked upon as gypsies and vagabonds.

The Church played as vital a part as the state in denouncing singing and dancing as well as the playing of instruments. However, in Ireland at this period the Church was aligned with the people. Nevertheless, the scarcity of harps and harpers at the Belfast Harp Festival of 1792 was not accidental. The harpers taking part in the festival represented the remnants of a dying tradition, strumming their harps and playing their modal music which seemed quaint and ancient to the ears of the eighteen-year-old trained organist, Edward Bunting, who was commissioned to note down the unfamiliar airs.

In the two centuries before 1792, polyphonic music, with its minor and major keys, had replaced modal music in continental Europe and in England. Bunting (1773–1843), who was later to become a famous collector of folk music in Ireland, was trained in polyphonic music and had to force the modal airs of the harpers into major and minor keys. Also present at the Harpers' Festival in Belfast was Wolfe Tone, who paid a quick visit and was not impressed, if one is to judge by his remark: 'Strum, strum, and be hanged.'

Though Bunting pioneered the rush to preserve what remained of the Gaelic airs, it was Thomas Moore in his *Irish Melodies* who popularised them. For a while it was fashionable among some purists to belittle Moore's efforts as 'sentimental productions suited to the drawing-rooms of the 19th century,' but, were it not for him, it is possible that none of those airs would have survived. I for one am convinced that Thomas Moore occupies an important place in the history of Anglo-Irish song, rescuing, as he did, many fine melodies from obscurity and injecting them with new life. His works fulfilled the needs of an increasingly English-speaking population in Ireland.

Moore himself is a very interesting person and led a fascinating life, mostly in England where he now lies buried. He was one of the first Catholics to be allowed to enter Dublin University after the law forbidding their attendance was amended. At university he dabbled briefly with nationalistic themes but was discouraged by the execution of his fellow student, Robert Emmet, who led an unsuccessful rebellion in Dublin in 1801.

Thomas Moore was not a rebel, though many of his songs were published in *The Nation*, the Young Ireland newspaper that influenced many generations of Irish nationalists. His poems came at a crucial period in the history of English-speaking Ireland and his songs were still very popular there in my youth. I first played the harp to take part in a school pageant based on Moore's life.

In Gaelic Ireland, the harp was associated with men, not women, and was used as an accompaniment for recitation. Harpers grew long nails which they used to pluck the wire-strung harps and a severe and devastating punishment for a harper was to have his nails cut off. Nowadays almost every harp is strung with gut or nylon and is plucked with the fingertips. In my young days the harp was not as fashionable in Ireland as it is today and fewer people played it.

A view of Glendalough, County Wicklow.

The Famine Song

Oh, the praties, they are small, over here,
    over here
Oh, the praties, they are small, over here.
Oh, the praties, they are small,
And we eat them skin and all
From the Spring until the Fall
Over here.

Oh, I wish that we were geese, night and
    morn, night and morn
Oh, I wish that we were geese, night and
    morn.
Oh, I wish that we were geese,
Then we all could be at peace
Till the time of our decease
Eating corn.

Oh, we're down into the dust, over here,
    over here,
Oh, we're down into the dust, over here.
Oh, we're down into the dust,
But the God in whom we trust
Will give us crumb for crust
Over here.

Where there is war there is often famine and, in the middle of the nineteenth century, an era where might was right, Ireland had its share of both. Civilians had little protection at a time when the scorched earth was a favourite instrument of war. Throughout history the colonising efforts of the successive waves of invaders brought famine to the dispossessed native citizenry – who found their fertile lands passing to foreign and often expatriate absentee landlords. Tenants had few rights except to surrender the cream of their crops to pay the rent and try to keep body and soul together on what was left – generally potatoes, or praties as they are called in this song. (*Prátai* is a Munster Gaelic word.)

While the potatoes were plentiful, the poorer people of rural Ireland managed to survive, but when the crops started to fail the rural population began to starve. In the summer of 1845 blight struck the potato crops and, within a few years, four million people (over half the population of Ireland), had perished from hunger. People in Ireland still talk about The Great Famine, or, in Gaelic, *An Gorta Mór*, one of the greatest preventable disasters that mankind has seen in modern times.

During the famine, Ireland became the staging point of the nineteenth-century Boat People – except that the boats were called 'coffin ships' because so few of them ever reached shore again. The route from Ireland to America was known as 'the skeleton way' because of the thousands of dead who were thrown overboard during the migration. 'If crosses and tombs could be erected on the water,' wrote one of the Commissioners for Emigration in the United States, '... the whole route of the emigrant vessels from Europe to America would long since have assumed the appearance of a crowded cemetery.' Because the government taxed

A woman of Inishere, Aran Islands, gazing out to sea. Hers is the next parish to America. Over the years hundreds of thousands of Irish men and women crossed the Atlantic with the result that today 24.4 per cent of Americans claim Irish ancestry.

the landlords for feeding the starving, landlords – often absentee themselves – found it cheaper to evict their tenants and pay some shipowner to carry them off penniless to the colonies. For example, it has been calculated that in 1847 alone, 100,000 starving emigrants – refugees – were shipped to North America from Ireland. Of those, 37,000 perished, 17,000 at sea and the rest on arrival in Canada. Considering the proportion of the population involved, the numbers of Vietnamese Boat People of today are small by comparison.

But, despite the appalling hazards, enough coffin ships crossed the Atlantic to lay the foundations of the Greater Ireland that exists today in the New World, and the descendants of the Boat People of nineteenth-century Ireland have served their adopted countries well. However, they did not find the climate sympathetic at first in their newly-adopted countries where customs were so very different from their own, as 'The Famine Song' demonstrates. The potatoes were smaller and the people ate them 'skin and all' – a practice to which the Irish of the last century were totally unaccustomed. For them, being forced to eat the skins was a sign of abject poverty and the unhappy lot of the 'almost starved'. Little did they know that the best part of the potato is next to the skin.

This period in history was one of great maritime activity in goods as well as in people. The English and Irish settlers in the New World brought with them a rich vein of folksong and so founded the whole culture of American traditional song, which has eventually become modern 'Country Music'. It was also the time which saw the development of the most vigorous song in the English tradition – the sea shanty – for this was the era of the clipper ships which sailed between English and American ports. Ireland was producing the great love and lyric songs of the Old World; Scotland had inherited the great epic and narrative ballads; England had the shanties, and Wales was enveloping itself in a peculiar genre more closely akin to art song and which is called 'penillion' – a curious and complex arrangement of voice and out-of-step accompaniment which sounds intriguing.

On the borders of Mayo and Connemara.

Sliabh Na mBan

The Mountain of the Women

Is oth liom féinig bualadh an lae úd
Do dhul ar Gaeil bhocht' 'sna céadta shlad;
Mar tá na méirlig ag déanamh game dinn
'S a' rá nach éinní leó pike no slea.
Nior tháinig ár Major i dtús an lae chughainn
Is ní rabhmar fhéin ann i gcóir ná 'gceart,
Ach mar sheólfai aoireacht de bha gan aoire,
Ar thaobh na gréine de Shliabh na mBan.

Tá'n Francach faobhrach 'sa loingeas gléasta,
Lé crannaibh géara 'ca ar muir le seal.
Is é sior scéal go bhfuil a dtriall ar Éirinn,
'S go gcuirfid Gaeil bhocht' arís 'na gceart.
Dá mba dhóigh liom féinneach go mb'fhior an scéal úd,
Bheadh mo chroidhe chomh héatrom lé lón ar sceach.
Go mbeadh claoi ar mhéirlig, 'san adhairc dá séide
Ar thaobh na gréine de Shliabh na mBan.

I dread the thought of that day's defeat
When the Gaels were slaughtered
For the invaders are mocking us
Claiming that they don't fear our lances or pikes.
To start with, our leader failed to turn up,
And we were unprepared in disarray
Driven like cattle without cowherd
On the sunny slopes of Sliabh na mBan.

The eager French are ready in their ships,
Tall masts sailing at sea for some time now.
It is rumoured that they're heading for Ireland
To restore their rights to the unfortunate Gael.
If I thought that such a story was true
My heart would be as light as a blackbird on the thorn;
That invaders would be vanquished and the horn would sound once more
On the sunny slopes of Sliabh na mBan.

'Sliabh na mBan' is a passionate cry from the heart, one of the great traditional songs of the Irish musical heritage. The words are full of heroic courage and pathos set to a very fine melody. It probably dates back to the end of the eighteenth century, but the song was revived at the turn of this century with the reawakening of a new wave of Irish nationalism. One of the characteristics of Irish classic folksong is its wide musical range. This has put it beyond the vocal capabilities of many singers and so risked its longevity.

Sliabh na mBan (literally 'the mountain of the women') is a mountain in the south of County Tipperary where a skirmish between a group of rebels and the local yeomanry took place during the rebellion of 1798. As the words of the song reveal, the rebels were ill-prepared and badly led, and so easily dispersed. But the poet takes heart from the rumour that the French are at sea sailing towards Ireland with help. In previous generations, before the French Revolution, the Irish looked to Spain for help and for a while to the deposed Stuarts but, in 1798, it was the turn of the French to be Ireland's allies – the privilege was accorded to

whoever was then at war with the government in London.

The mountain of *Sliabh na mBan*, which is over 2,300 feet high, is clearly visible to those travelling the road between Kilkenny and Clonmel. It is just north of Carrick-on-Suir, a town I visited once to see some friends. What strikes me most about all those Irish country towns is the wealth of tradition which they harbour. Carrick-on-Suir is no different; Carrick Castle, an Elizabethan fortified mansion, is the only one of its kind in Ireland. This castle was one of the seats of the Butlers, earls and later dukes of Ormonde, who played a major part in British government in Ireland for four centuries. The story goes that Carrick Castle was built specially by the tenth Earl of Ormonde to receive his cousin, Queen Elizabeth I – a visit she never made. Dermod O'Hurley, the archbishop of Cashel, martyred in Dublin in 1584, once sought refuge in Carrick Castle but was, nevertheless, arrested, despite the protest of the then earl.

Wherever I travel in Ireland, I like to stop in the smaller towns to learn something about the history of the surrounding countryside. It helps immensely if one is travelling with someone well-versed in such matters and then a simple journey from A to B becomes an interesting and painless excursion into history.

Blarney Castle at sunset. A MacCarthy fortress that withstood several sieges between the 15th and 17th centuries. Nowadays famous for its Blarney Stone reputed to bestow the gift of eloquence on those who kiss it.

A couple of years ago I travelled all over Ireland giving school recitals for the Music Association of Ireland and, for the first time in my life, was able to take a more leisurely look at the Irish countryside. I found, and still find, that in the smaller towns, and in the areas surrounding them, there are such numerous relics of the past that one could spend hours on end immersed in the contemplation of history and, if one were so disposed, perhaps imbibing salutary lessons from it. It is all there – one man's wisdom and another man's folly, carved into the countryside, chronicled with ruined castles and churches as though discarded games on the chessboard of time. Unlike the larger population centres of modern Ireland, rural Ireland has no need for museums to remind one of the past. It is indeed a living museum for anyone with any sense of history.

The thread connecting the songs in this chapter has been chiefly historical. But countrymen are credited with being equally at home with fact and fancy, so it is not inappropriate to follow with a chapter on myth and the supernatural. What better title for such a mixture than 'The Fairy Tree'.

Chapter III

Silent O Moyle

Silent O Moyle! be the roar of thy water,
Break not, ye breezes, your chain of repose,
While murmuring mournfully, Lir's lonely daughter
Tells to the night-star her tale of woes.
When shall the swan, her death-note singing,
Sleep, with wings in darkness furl'd?
When will heaven, its sweet bell ringing,
Call my spirit from this stormy world.

Sadly, O Moyle! to thy winter wave weeping,
Fate bids me languish long ages away!
Yet still in her darkness doth Erin lie sleeping,
Still doth the pure light its dawning delay!
When will that day-star, mildly springing,
Warm our isle with peace and love?
When will heaven, its sweet bell ringing,
Call my spirit to the fields above?

'Silent O Moyle' is called The Song of Fionnuala in Moore's *Irish Melodies*. Fionnuala was the eldest of the four children of Lir, king of the Tuatha Dé Dannan people in the mythological folklore of ancient Ireland. The names of her three brothers were Conn, Aedh and Fiachra. The story of the Children of Lir must be one of the most heart-rending tales of cruelty and enchantment in all mythology. Each time I read it I'm moved to tears.

Briefly, the story tells how the children were transformed into swans by their jealous stepmother, Aoife, who was also their aunt. The spell condemns them to live as swans for the next thousand years, 300 years to be spent by Lake Derravarragh, 300 on the sea of Moyle – that savage and treacherous stretch of narrow water dividing Antrim from Scotland – and a final 300 years or so on the west coast of Ireland. Not until the coming of Christianity would the spell be broken by the sound of the Mass bell.

The evil stepmother, Aoife, allowed the children to retain their human intellect and speech and she also gave them the power to sing with such sweetness that all those who heard them never wanted to listen to any other music. After hundreds of years of indescribable suffering and hardship, these gentle creatures were eventually befriended by a Christian monk called Caemhach, who talked to them and told them the story of Christ. News of the marvellous talking and singing swans spread and one day the reigning queen of Ireland, a vain and covetous woman, heard about them. She wished to possess them and ordered that they should be taken to her, by force if necessary. However, as the swans were being dragged away, Caemhach's Mass bell rang out, and instantly the four comely swans regained human form; no longer bright and beautiful children but now ancient, withered humans. They begged the monk for baptism and, having received it, died peacefully. After they died, Caemhach, prompted to look upwards, was moved by a strange vision of four lovely children, their faces radiant with unutterable joy.

The air to 'Silent O Moyle' was sent to Thomas Moore by George Petrie (1789–1866). O'Sullivan ranks the tune as one of the finest used by Moore in his *Irish Melodies*.

The Fairy Tree

1. All night around the thorn tree
    The Little People play;
    And men and women passing
    Will turn their heads away.
    From break of dawn till moonrise
    Alone it stands on high,
    With twisted springs for branches
    Across the winter sky.

2. They'll tell you dead men hung there,
    Its black and bitter fruit,
    To guard the buried treasure
    Round which it twines its root.
    They'll tell you Cromwell hung them,
    But that could never be;
    He'd be in dread like others
    To touch the Fairy Tree.

3. But Katie Ryan saw there
    In some sweet dream she had,
    The Blessed Son of Mary
    And all His face was sad.
    She dreamt she heard Him saying:
    'Why should they be afraid?
    Why should they be afraid?
    When from a branch of thorn tree
    The crown I wore was made?'

4. From moonrise round the thorn tree
    The Little People play;
    And men and women passing
    Will turn their heads away.
    But if your heart's a child's heart
    And if your eyes are clean,
    You'll never fear the thorn tree
    That grows beyond Clogheen.

The realm of the spirit has interested me as long as I can remember. As a committed Christian I nurture within myself a profound belief in the supernatural. My fascination with what I call the preternatural fairy world and with mythology generally, is also strong. Some of my favourite writers, people like C. S. Lewis and J. R. Tolkien, have the gift of writing about the interpenetration of the supernatural and mythological worlds in such a way that the receptive reader finds not only his imagination kindled, but also his spirit enriched and invigorated.

Tolkien's great myth, *The Lord of the Rings*, is such a favourite of mine that I've called the seventeenth-century thatched cottage where I live, Rivendell. Greek mythology too claimed my interest from an early age, as did the folktales and sagas of my native land; and when I go to some small Greek island for my annual holiday, I usually arm myself with books of both Greek and Irish myths.

Tolkien said that, just as speech is invention about objects and ideas, so myth is invention about truth. He believed firmly in the inherent truth of myths: they reflect something of the true light, the Truth that is with God. Man needs myth, for the same reason that a world, small enough for our understanding, would not be large enough for our needs. The Irish in particular understand this need instinctively, natural storytellers that many of them are. James Stephens has provided us with a wonderful myth in his many-faceted book, *The Crock of Gold*. James Stephens (poet and writer, a Dubliner and of the same vintage as James Joyce), was one of the major figures of the Irish literary Rennaissance at the beginning of this century. When Christianity came to Ireland in 432 it was embraced relatively quickly by the people and it took root without ousting the ancient beliefs that were as old as the race itself. Many of these beliefs survive to the present day. For instance, in my young days I saw people putting milk out at night for the fairies and then going off to Mass next morning and seeing nothing incongruous in such behaviour.

By temperament, the Irish move easily through the different levels of reality, for are they not 'the music-makers and the dreamer of dreams'? W. B. Yeats recalls William Morris comparing the Norse and Irish accounts of the battle of Clontarf (1014) which ended Norse power in Ireland. The Norseman was interested in how things were done but the Irishman turned aside as if bored by so dull a business and started to describe beautiful supernatural events. The Irish storyteller's imagination is always running off to *Tír na nóg*, the Land of Eternal Youth, the realm of fantasy, where everything has a hidden meaning. This is how an ordinary and crooked thorn bush could become the Fairy Tree.

In this song, theology, myth and history are imaginatively intertwined to form a new creation. There is an abundance of dolmens, cromlechs, ogham stones, plundered abbeys, ruined castles and memories of battles long ago to feed the popular imagination. The children see these relics of the past. Daily they pass them by on their way to and from school. They do not have to imagine them. They are in constant living touch with them and require no books to help their imagination.

I remember my grandfather telling us children about his encounters with fairies as he cycled home along a lonely stretch of road in County Sligo very late on moonlit nights. Even now I don't know to what extent he believed these stories himself, but they were very real to us, and he was careful to teach us a healthy respect for the fairy fort or *rath* near his home. Grandfather, we were told, 'knew' when there was an imminent death in the family – he was warned by means of a knocking sound under his pillow.

Yeats wrote that certain areas around Sligo were 'very noted fairy localities' and he refers to some of these places in his 'The Stolen Child' (p. 103). Old men and children seem to be the ones best-attuned to the fairy world. As Yeats described them: 'those who have not felt the pressure of mere daylight existence and those with whom it is growing less'. Fairies are sometimes referred to as *Na Daoine Maithe*, or, the Good People, and, because of the frequent reference to them in this chapter, a word or two by way of introduction is in order.

In Irish mythology and folklore, there are two classes of fairies: the sociable and the solitary. Among the sociable fairies there are the plebs and the aristocrats. The 'ordinary' fairies, the *sídheóg* or wee folk, go about their daily tasks plying different trades as we mortals do. These are the Little People who haunt the sacred thorn bushes and the green *raths* that dot the Irish countryside. Apart from occasionally stealing a child, and leaving in its place a withered fairy or 'changeling', their habits are good. They frequently play pranks but, as a rule, are kind to

Poulnabrone Dolmen, County Clare, is one of the better examples of the portal dolmens in which megalithic man buried his dead.

the good and bad to the wicked. Then there are the tall, beautiful *sídhe* who live in the hollow hills and who move so majestically and hauntingly through the work of W. B. Yeats.

The solitary fairies, on the other hand, are not such as humans would relish meeting – with the exception, perhaps, of the leprechaun. He is a mischievous little fellow, full of tricks and we will meet him again in another song. We will also come across the *bean sídhe* again and we have already seen what the *leanán sídhe* could get up to. We can skip the rest of the solitary fairies – the *púca*, the *fear gorta* and the *dullahan* – for they do not appear in any of the songs.

Some people believed that fairies were fallen angels, not good enough to be allowed into heaven and not bad enough to be sent to hell. They were condemned to roam the earth till the end of time. However, on the night of Hallowe'en, the eve of All Saints, they were permitted special liberties. Then they celebrated with wild revelling, filling their fairy music with such enchantment that anyone who heard it was never the same again.

In order to keep children indoors on this dangerous night parents devised various games which gave rise to Hallowe'en parties. If however a child did have to leave home on this night, its parents took extra precautions like dressing boys in girls' clothing (for some reason fairies were not interested in girls), hence the custom of masquerading around the streets on Hallowe'en. In Gaelic such masqueraders were referred to as *mac soipín*, literally 'descendant of sop' – sop being a Gaelic word for 'straw' and also for the 'whirlwind' which was popularly believed to be but a group of the Good People on the rampage. In many parts of Ireland boys wore petticoats until they reached school-going age, a practice less connected perhaps with easing nappy changing than with a belief in the fairies' fondness of little boys.

So much for the Little People mentioned in the 'Fairy Tree'. Like the Blessed Son of Mary, they represent a benign influence. Not so Cromwell, who, for good reason, always figures as someone less than lovable in Irish history and folklore. For a person to invoke 'the curse of Cromwell' on another was to wish that person the worst possible mishap. In 1649 Cromwell came to Ireland and his first act was to put the town of Drogheda to the sword, man, woman and child. It was a foretaste of things to come. Having divided most of the fertile land of the country among his followers, and with the fate of Drogheda as a salutary warning, he gave the native Irish the choice of going 'to hell or to Connacht', banishing them to the barren lands west of the River Shannon. Unlike the fairies, the native Irish were, in Cromwell's opinion, bad enough to be sent to hell but most of them preferred to postpone the day and risk Connacht instead.

Clogheen, mentioned in the song, is in County Tipperary on the scenic Vee Road that winds its way through to the Knockmealdown Gap, a well-known tourist attraction. Not far away are the famous Mitchelstown Caves containing some of the finest examples of subterranean formations in Ireland. It was in one of those caves that the 'Sugán Earl' of Desmond, with a large price on his head, took refuge in 1601. 'Sugán' is the Gaelic word for a rope made of straw. It is not surprising that Cromwell appears in local folklore and song, because the whole of this area saw much activity during the Cromwellian campaign in Ireland. It was at Clonmel that Cromwell met his most severe setback and it was at Cahir Castle, also in the same area in the valley of the Suir, that the Cromwellian war was officially declared over in 1652.

Dé Luain Dé Máirt

*Bhí Dónall bocht Cam, go raibh dronn ar a
  dhrom,*
Ag gabháil tríd in ngleann ins an oíche,
Nuair a chuala sé ceól bog binn na sióg
Ag teacht chuige 'r leirigh na gaoithe –
Dé Luain, Dé Máirt, Dé Luain, Dé Máirt,
Dé Luain, Dé Máirt . . .

Do stad sé 'gus d'eist go ciúin le gach séis,
Is i ngeibheann an ghlé-bhinnis bhí se;
*Ach a chroi 'stig do breodhadh, mar theip ar an
  gceól,*
Is níor cuireadh crioch cóir leis an líne.
Dé Luain, Dé Máirt, Dé Luain, Dé Máirt,
Dé Luain, Dé Máirt . . .

*Do ghlac Donall Cam, go raibh dronn ar a
  dhrom,*
Misneach, is do chan go deas séimh caoin –
Dé Luain, Dé Máirt, Dé Luain, Dé Máirt,
Dé Luain, Dé Máirt is Dé Céadaoin.
Dé Luain, Dé Máirt, Dé Luain, Dé Máirt,
Dé Luain, Dé Máirt is Dé Céadaoin.

*Nuair a chuala 'n slua sidhe an chrioch gheal
  fhirbhinn –*
Nach orthu bhí an ríméad 's an t-áthas;
Do bhain siad an dronn de Dgónall bocht Cam
Is d'imigh sé abhaile gan mhacail.
Dé Luain, Dé Máirt, Dé Luain, Dé Máirt,
Dé Luain, Dé Máirt is Dé Céadaoin.

Monday Tuesday

Poor crooked Dónal who had a hump on
  his back
Was travelling through the glen one night
When he heard the soft gentle music of the
  fairies
Coming to him on the wings of the wind,
  singing
Monday, Tuesday, Monday, Tuesday.
Monday, Tuesday.

He paused and listened quietly to every
  strain,
Enthralled by the wondrous sweetness.
But his heart was startled for the music
  stopped
Without achieving a graceful ending to
  the tune
Monday, Tuesday, Monday, Tuesday.
Monday, Tuesday.

Crooked Dónal, who had a hump on his
  back,
Took courage and gently sang
Monday, Tuesday, Monday, Tuesday.
Monday, Tuesday and Wednesday.
Monday, Tuesday, Monday, Tuesday.
Monday, Tuesday and Wednesday.

When the fairy host heard this musical
  ending,
They were exceedingly pleased and
  delighted;
They removed the hump from poor
  crooked Dónal,
And he departed home without blemish.
Monday, Tuesday, Monday, Tuesday.
Monday, Tuesday and Wednesday.

The story of '*Dé Luain, Dé Máirt*' is told eloquently in the song itself. In the folklore of south Tipperary, where the song comes from, there is a sequel to the story of Dónal. News of the hunchback's good fortune soon spread and, eventually, reached the ears of another hunchback named Jack Madden, an altogether less amiable character than Dónal. After making all the necessary enquiries, Madden journeyed to the fairy moat and heard the music as expected, together with Dónal's own addition. However, being an insensitive and impatient man, and more interested in disposing of his own hump than adding anything to the music, he rudely interrupted the song to add '*Diardaoin*' or 'Thursday' to the end of the verse. But, as this did not enhance the music in any way, the fairies were furious and, having given Madden a thrashing, they picked up Dónal's discarded hump and placed it on Madden's back along with his own. Needless to say, that about finished Jack Madden and he died shortly afterwards.

Folklore identifies the spot where the incident of Dónal and the fairies took place: it was at the great Motte of Knockgraffon, a prominent landmark four miles north of Cahir in County Tipperary. It is said to have been the coronation place of the Munster kings before the seat of the dynasty was moved to Cashel in 370. Later on, the Anglo-Normans made Knockgraffon their headquarters, building there a stronghold from which they commanded an important ford crossing the River Suir. Adjoining the motte is the ruin of a sixteenth-century castle belonging to the Butlers and in the old graveyard nearby are the remains of the church where Friar Geofrey Keating, one of the famous Four Masters, preached the sermon which led to his being outlawed. So all the ingredients are here at Knockgraffon to invite a powerful fairy presence.

Seóithín Seó

A bhean úd thíos ar bhruach an tsrutháin,
  Seóithín seó seóthúló!
An dtuigeann tusa fáith mo ghearáin?
  Seóithín seó seóthúló!
'S gur bliain 's lá inniu fuaduiodh me óm leanán,
  Seóithín seó seóthúló!
'S do rugú isteach me i Lios an Chnocáin.
  Seóithín seó seóthúló!

CHORUS   *Seóithín seóithín, seóithín seóithín,*
          Seóithín seó seóthúló;
          Seóithín seóithín, seóithín seóithín,
          Seóithín seó seóthúló.

Abair lem' chéile teacht amáireach,
  Seóithín seó seóthúló!
Scian coise duibhe a thabhairt na láimh leis,
  Seóithín seó seóthúló!
'S an choinneal chéireach i gcroi a dheárnan,
  Seóithín seó seóthúló!
'S an capall tosaigh a bhualadh sa mbearnain.
  Seóithín seó seóthúló!

CHORUS

Seóithín Seó

O woman yonder by the stream,
Seóithín seó, seóthúló
Do you understand why I complain,
Seóithín seó, seóthúló?
For a year and a day ago today, I was spirited
  away from my lover
And brought into the fairy mound of Cnocan.

Tell my husband to come tomorrow,
Seóithín seó, seóthúló,
A blackhandled knife to bring in his hand,
Seóithín seó, seóthúló.
A wax candle in his fist
And the first horse he meets in the gap.

This song is sometimes known by its first line, 'O Woman Yonder'. It tells the story of a mortal mother spirited away from her family by the fairies and held captive in the fairy fort nursing fairy babies. The phrase *'seóithín seó'* is roughly the equivalent of 'rockaby baby' in English. One day, while the captive mother is nursing her fairy baby outside the fort, she spies an erstwhile neighbour of hers across the stream. She relates her plight to this woman and passes on information about the three elements her husband must bring with him if he is to break the enchantment. Between each line she rocks the fairy infant, singing gently *seóithín seó* as much to continue the lullaby as to deceive any listening fairies as to her real activity.

The three elements mentioned in the song are universal antidotes to magic spells. The knife: iron is repellent to evil. Many people keep a rusty nail or a horseshoe above their doors to ward off the advances of malign spiritual forces. Horseshoes were nailed to doorposts, open side up, to trap evil which was supposed to travel in circles. If the open end of the horseshoe was facing down, it was thought that the evil could fall to the earth and find itself a victim. Candles: they are omnipresent in folklore, as indeed in religious ceremony, as much for their symbolism as for their practical usage. The horse: the first horse coming through the gap would obviously be the leader and was always ridden by the chief of the fairies. Horses and magic often went together, just as horseshoes had magical powers.

Sweet Child of Glory

Sweet child of glory come down to us here from heaven,
To bring us the peace that the world cannot understand;
My heart is amazed that you, humble, should lie in the cold,
When you are the Saviour who hold the whole world in your hand.

O look at the children of Érin who are coming to you,
Like angels and shepherds that came on that night long ago;
Most holy the name that we praise, the name of our God,
Oh, take our thanksgiving like warmth in the cold of the snow.

We beg of you, Jesus, behold us and bring us your peace,
Bring peace to a world that is shaken with evil and strife;
And comfort your people in time of despairing and grief,
Bring peace to your children, O Lord, and giver of life.

Sweet Child of Glory is a translation of a Gaelic hymn '*Na Leanaí i mBeithil*' made for me by my friend the late George Scott-Moncrief. Literally translated, the Gaelic title means 'The Children in Bethlehem' and it is a straightforward prayer that is sometimes used as a carol. It is strange that the tradition of carol-singing does not appear to have existed in Ireland at all. The absence of this custom may have an historical explanation – the practice of the Catholic religion was suppressed for so long – but there is no record of carol-singing even in the ancient Gaelic tradition.

Muire Mhór

Is maith an bhean Muire Mhór,
Màthair Árd-Ri na Slógh Sior;
Siad a grásta is gnáth lán –
Bean do chuir fál fo gach tír.

Bean í dá gclaonann ceart,
Bean is mó neart is brí,
Bean is buige fá ór dearg,
Bean le gcoisctear fearg an Rí.

Bean do bheir radharc do dháll,
Bean is treise tháll ar Neamh,
Bean do thóg mo náimhde dhíom,
Bean is díon dom ar gach cath.

Great Mary

Great Mary is a good woman
Mother of the High King of the Eternal Hosts.
Her favours are for ever plentiful,
A woman who protects each land.

A woman to whom justice is attracted,
A woman of immense power,
A woman most generous with precious gifts,
A woman by whom the anger of the king is restrained.

A woman who gives sight to the blind,
A woman most powerful in heaven,
A woman who defends me from my enemies,
A woman who protects me against temptation.

This Gaelic hymn to the Mother of God is part of a much longer poem written by Eoghan O'Duffy, a Franciscan Friar from Ulster. It was written in response to the preaching of Myler MacGrath (Maolmhuire Mac Craith), a former Catholic

bishop whom Queen Elizabeth I appointed Protestant Archbishop of Cashel in 1571. Maolmhuire, MacGrath's christian name, literally means 'servant of Mary' and this lent a certain poignancy to the poem if not the man, which would not have been lost on the listeners. It is interesting that *Muire*, which is another form of the name Mary, is in Gaelic strictly reserved for the Mother of God and is never given to any other woman – much the same as in English Jesus is not given as a name for boys. *Maoiliosa* or 'the servant of Jesus' is frequently used in old Gaelic as a man's name.

The see of Cashel, to which MacGrath was appointed archbishop, was at one time the most important see in Munster. The Rock of Cashel is a most imposing outcrop of limestone rising 200 feet out of the level fertile plain beside the River Suir. It is crowned with a magnificent collection of historic ruins and is such a distinctive landmark that it is not surprising that the kings of Munster made it their seat from 370 until 1101 when King Murtagh O'Brien granted it to the Church. Saint Patrick visited the Rock in 450, and the legendary Brian Boru, who defeated the Danes at Clontarf (1014), was crowned King of Munster there. A cathedral built on the rock in 1169 was burnt down in 1495 by Gerald, Earl of Kildare. The excuse he later gave to the English King, Henry VII, was that he thought the bishop was inside!

One would need to spend many more hours than I had at my disposal at the Rock of Cashel to appreciate fully its historical and archaeological significance – just as some acquaintance with the era of Myler MacGrath is necessary for the proper appreciation of the Gaelic hymn to the Mother of God.

OPPOSITE *The Rock of Cashel. Rising 200 feet above the Munster plain, this rock is one of Ireland's most remarkable historic sites. Seat of the Munster kings from 370 to 1101 when King Murtagh O'Brien granted it to the Church – less out of devotion than from a desire to deprive his rivals of a headquarters with symbolic rallying powers. In 1169 a cathedral was built on top of the rock but this was burnt down in 1495 by the Earl of Kildare who excused his action by saying that he thought that the bishop was inside.*

Deus Meus

Deus meus adjuva me,
Tiúir dom do shearc a Mhic dhil Dé;
Tiúir dom do shearc, a Mhic dhil Dé,
Deus meus adjuva me.

Domina da quod peto a te –
Tiúir dom go dian, a ghrian ghlan ghlé.

Tuum amorem sicut vis –
Tiúir dom go tréan a déarfad arís.

Domine, Domine exaudi me –
M'anam a bheith lán ded ghrá, a Dhé.

My God

My God help me.
Give me your love bright Son of God.
My God help me.
Give me your love bright Son of God.

Lord, give me what I beg for,
Give me in plenty O Sun-like one.

If it is your wish that I love you,
Be generous to me, I repeat;

Lord, Lord, hear me,
Make my soul full of your love, O God.

'*Deus Meus*' is yet another of the songs I learnt from Seán Óg. The words are by Maol-Iosa O'Brolchain who died in 1086. There is a copy of the song in the *Book of Lismore* and another in *Lámhscríbhín Ui Mhurchú*, now in Maynooth College.

Scribes who wanted to test their new quills sometimes tried them out on the wide margins of the manuscripts they were working on. The result showed not only the quality of the pens but, from time to time, an unexpected skill at versifying, as well as a lively wit. When the manuscripts were trimmed at the edges before binding, it usually meant the loss of these marginal verses but, fortunately, '*Deus Meus*' survived, and it is believed to be one of the loveliest of those preserved. The plain chant-like melody matches the beauty of the words but, sadly, the author is unknown.

Some Irish manuscripts are very old. In ancient Ireland, they were regarded as valuable possessions and disputes about ownership could be the cause of battles, such as the Battle of Dromcath or the 'battle of the books', fought at Cuildrevne near my home town of Sligo, in 561, between the followers of Saint Columcille and Saint Finian. As far as I know, it is the first recorded battle over copyright, other than those fought by lawyers.

If I were allowed my pick of Irish mementos for a Desert Island Discs situation, I think I would opt for a collection of ancient Irish manuscripts, preferably with the notes on the margins intact! Two other manuscripts that I know of have associations with my home county of Sligo; one is the *Book of Ballymote* compiled in the Franciscan Friary at Ballymote in 1391, and the other is a copy of the Psalms made by Columcille – both of these are now held in the Royal Irish Academy in Dublin.

OPPOSITE *The round tower at Glendalough. A thousand years ago Glendalough was one of Ireland's four centres of pilgrimage – the others being Downpatrick, Croagh Patrick and Patrick's Purgatory on Lough Derg. It is nowadays a popular beauty spot.*

The Leprechaun

In a shady nook one moonlight night,
    a leprechaun I spied;
With scarlet cap and coat of green,
    a *crúiscín* by his side.
'Twas tick! tack! tick! his hammer went
    upon a weeny shoe,
And I laughed to think of a purse of gold
But the fairy was laughing too!...

With tiptoe step and beating heart quite
    softly I drew nigh;
There was mischief in his merry face,
    a twinkle in his eye.
He hammered and sang with tiny voice and
    drank his mountain dew,
Oh! I laughed to think he was caught at last,
But the fairy was laughing too!...

As quick as thought I seized the elf: 'Your
    fairy purse,' I cried.
'The purse,' he said, ''tis in her hand, that
    lady by your side.'
I turned to look – the elf was off! – and what
    was I to do?
Oh, I laughed to think what a fool I'd been;
And the fairy was laughing too!...

OPPOSITE *Glencar waterfall, about 7 miles north of Sligo. When I was a child the family went to Glencar for picnics.*

The air to the 'Leprechaun' is traditional and the words are by Dr Patrick V. Joyce.

James Stephens wrote that a 'leprechaun without a pot of gold is like a rose without perfume, a bird without a wing, or an inside without an outside'. *Crúiscín* is Gaelic for crock, and Stephens in his book *The Crock of Gold* lets one leprechaun explain to Séamus Beg and Bríd Beg how they acquired their gold: 'In the night time we go about the country into people's houses and we clip little pieces off their money and so, bit by bit, we get a crock of gold together, because, do you see, a leprechaun has to have a crock of gold so that if he's captured by men folk he may be able to ransom himself.'

No figure in Irish mythology or folklore is better known internationally than the leprechaun. It seems that the Irish carried him with them everywhere. In the Collins English Dictionary he falls between leporine and leprosarium and is defined as a mischievous elf often believed to have a treasure hoard. The song gives a pretty good idea of the roguish and cunning nature of this rather likeable little fairy who is generally pictured sitting under a tree, mending a shoe without a care in the world. If anyone who sees a leprechaun steadfastly keeps his eye on him, he can force the little miser to surrender his crock of gold; but no one that I know of, has, so far, succeeded.

The Stolen Child

1. Where dips the rocky highland
   Of Sleuth Wood in the lake,
   There lies a leafy island
   Where flappy herons wake
   The drowsy water-rats.
   There we've hid our fairy vats
   Full of berries,
   And of reddest stolen cherries.
   Come away, O, human child!
   To the woods and waters wild
   With a fairy hand in hand,
   For the world's more full of weeping than
       you can understand.

2. Where the wave of moonlight glosses
       The dim grey sands with light,
   Far off by farthest Rosses
       We foot it all the night,
   Weaving olden dances,
   Mingling hands, and mingling glances,
       Till the moon has taken flight;

3. To and fro we leap,
       And chase the frothy bubbles,
       While the world is full of troubles.
   And is anxious in its sleep.
   Come away! O, human child!
   To the woods and waters wild,
   With a fairy hand in hand,
   For the world's more full of weeping than
       you can understand.

4. Where the wandering water gushes
       From the hills above Glen-Car,
   In pools among the rushes,
       That scarce could bathe a star,
   We seek for slumbering trout,
       And whispering in their ears;
         We give them evil dreams,
   Leaning softly out
       From ferns that drop their tears
         Of dew on the young streams.
   Come, Come away, O human child!
   To the woods and waters wild,
   With a fairy hand in hand,
   For the world's more full of weeping than
       you can understand.

5. Away with us, he's going,
       The solemn-eyed;
   He'll hear no more the lowing
       Of the calves on the warm hill-side.
   Or the kettle on the hob
       Sing peace into his breast;
   Or see the brown mice bob
       Round and round the oatmeal chest.
   For he comes, the human child,
   To the woods and waters wild,
   With a fairy hand in hand,
   For the world's more full of weeping than
       he can understand.

The Stolen Child was written by W. B. Yeats and set to music by Áine Nic Gabhann. Yeats spent part of his youth in Sligo and his sojourn there had a permanent influence on him and on his work. The countryside near Sligo town and around Lough Gill is known today as 'the Yeats country'. Some of the places mentioned in 'The Stolen Child' are familiar names of my childhood days: Sleuth Wood, Rosses, Glencar. I remember picnics with my family beside Glencar waterfall; it is good fairy country around Sligo.

West of Sligo is the county's main natural feature, the Hill of Knocknarea, literally the Hill of the Kings, 1,078 feet high, with a fine panoramic view from its summit. Not far away is Carrowmore, a low hill possessing the largest group of

megalithic remains in these islands – dolmens, stone circles, and cairns with sepulchral chambers. It was while travelling the lonely stretch of road past Carrowmore that my grandfather claimed the fairies tried to pull him off his bicycle.

Nearby at Cloverhill is another sepulchral monument with carvings which are thought to be Bronze Age (1900–500 BC). On the summit of Knocknarea is a gigantic cairn known as Miscaun Meadhbh, or Maeve's Mound, or, simply, Queen Maeve's grave. This is regarded traditionally as commemorating Queen Maeve of Connacht who flourished here in the first century of the Christian era. The cairn itself is 630 feet around the base, 80 feet high, and 100 feet diameter at the top. All this and more was good material for the Yeatsian fairy world.

From myth and the supernatural we now move on to songs for (and about) children. After all, according to Yeats, children, like old people are supposed to be better able to 'see' spirits, particularly the fairy. I call the next chapter 'The Castle of Dromore', a favourite song of mine that touches on the supernatural, the *sidhe*, and the link between the two.

'Come away, o human child!
To the woods and waters wild.'

Chapter IV

The Castle of Dromore

October winds lament around the castle of Dromore,
Yet peace is in her lofty halls a *pháiste bheag a stor*.
Though autumn leaves may droop and die,
A bud of spring are you. Singing
Hushaba lúla lú-ló-lán, sing *hushaba-lú-la-ló*.

May no ill winds hinder us, my helpless babe and me,
Dread spirit of the Blackwater, Clan Owen's wild banshee;
And holy Mary pitying us in heaven for grace doth sue. Singing
Hushaba lula lú-ló-lán, sing *hushaba-lú-la-ló*.

A Róis mo chroí, a shlaitín óir
As gardha drom an óir
Bí a' fás go mbeidh gach cleite bheag
Mar scíathan iolra mhóir;
Is léim annsan ar fúd an tsaoil,
Oibri is saori clú. Seinam
Hushaba lúla lú-ló-lán, seinam hushaba-lú-la-ló.

At a time in Irish history when English was replacing Gaelic as the common language of the people, there were many songs, like this lullaby, which used both tongues. '*A pháiste beag mo stór*', means 'little child, my treasure', while the last verse translates as: 'Rose of my heart, golden rod from the garden of Drom an Óir, may you grow till each little feather becomes like a great eagle's wing, and may you then leap all over the world, making a name for yourself.' Here we see again the curious interweaving of Christian piety and folk mythology which seems to come so naturally to the Celt, and which can be so deeply satisfying to the human spirit.

The banshee (*bean sídhe*) is one of the solitary fairies. Many of the great families of Ireland had their banshee. Her wail was said to presage a death in that family. I remember one night in Sligo when I was a small child, not more than two or three years old, when the silence was suddenly shattered by a spine-chilling cry outside in the fields; I was told it was the banshee. How comforting it was then to feel safe in my little cot, where I could snuggle down under the blanket and shut out that truly terrible cry.

The river Blackwater, mentioned in the song, enters the sea at Youghal. It rises in the Galtee Mountains, where we have already found Dónal the hunchback having his encounter with the friendly fairies who removed the hump from his back. The 'Castle of Dromore' was one of the earliest songs I learnt to sing, accompanying myself on the Celtic harp.

Haigh Didil Dum

Haigh didil dum, an cat is a mháthair
D' imigh go Gaillimh a' marcaíocht ar bhárdal;

CHORUS   *Haigh didil dum, agus haigh didil dero,*
Is haigh didil didil di haigh didil dum.

Haigh didil dum, do tháinig an bháisteach,
Hóbair go mbáifí an cat is a mháthair,

CHORUS

Haigh didil dum thug Walter dinéar dóibh,
Dreóilin beag rósta, 'gus smóilin is céirseach.

CHORUS

Haigh didil dum, the cat and his mother
Went to Galway riding on a drake.

CHORUS

Haigh didil dum, down came the rain;
The cat and his mother were nearly drowned.

CHORUS

Walter gave them dinner,
A little roast wren, a lark and a thrush.

An Caitín Bán

Bhí an caitín glas ag siúl go deas
Nuair a fuair sí a maicín sínte,
'S gur bliain ón lá san fuair sí a clann
Caite is báite i dtrínse.

CHORUS   *An caitín bán, bán, bán*
          An caitín bán, cat Bhríde,
          An caitín bán, sneachta bán,
          Do báithiú ins an dtrínse.

D'eirigh an mháithrín suas 'na seasamh,
Nuair a fuair sí a maicín sínte;
Thug si abhaile é is rinne si leaba,
A's thosuigh si annsin dhá chaoine.

CHORUS

Ba ghlas i a shúil 's ba dheas a shiúl,
'S a choisméig lúthmhar éatrom;
Is measa liom siúd ag dul faoi'n úir,
Ná cúige Mumhan dá éisteacht.

CHORUS

Bhí cruit ar dhruim an chaitín bháin
Chomh mór le jug trí phionta,
'S nár dheas an show ag daoine móra
An caitín Pól deas Bhríde.

CHORUS

The Little White Kitten

The grey cat was daintily out walking
When she came upon her son dead.
It was a year to the day when she
          discovered her family
Cast in a ditch and drowned.

CHORUS   Dear little kitten
          Bridget's white kitten
          Snow-white kitten
          Drowned in a ditch

The little mother stood up
When she found her kitten dead.
She brought him home and made a bed,
And commenced there to mourn him.

CHORUS

His eye was grey, his gait was dainty,
His footstep fast and light.
It hurts me more to have to bury him
Than all of Munster together.
Munster together.

CHORUS

The little white kitten had a hump on his back
As big as a three-pint jug.
It was the delight of grownups
Pol, Bridget's little kitten.

My friend Sarah Hook, who often travels with me on tours, has taught me much about animals. Recently she reminded me of an exchange she overheard me having with some member of the audience who had come backstage after a concert. Apparently this particular person was a keen animal-lover and was happily remarking on the number of nature songs and songs about animals in my repertoire. She enquired if I, by any chance, had a song about a cat.

'Yes, indeed,' I'm reported to have said enthusiastically, 'I have a beautiful song about a cat.' I was referring to '*An Caitín Bán*'.

By now my visitor's interest was visibly aroused. 'I love cats,' she said, 'please do tell me more about the song.'

'Yes, I sang it in a competition when I was eight. I remember it well because I fell off the stage. As a matter of fact,' I continued cheerily, 'the song is about a dead cat.'

And there, rather abruptly, the conversation ended.

The Gartan Mother's Lullaby

1. Sleep, O babe, for the red bee hums
    The silent twilight's fall.
    Aoibheall from the Grey Rock comes
    To wrap the world in thrall.
    A *leanbhan o*, my child, my joy,
    My love and heart's desire;
    The crickets sing you lullaby,
    Beside the dying fire.

2. Dusk is drawn, and the Green Man's thorn
    Is wreathed in rings of joy;
    Síobhra sails his boat till morn
    Upon the starry bog.
    A *leanbhan o*, the paly moon,
    Hath brimm'd her cusp in dew
    And weeps to hear the sad sleep tune I sing,
    O love to you.

3. Sleep, O babe, for the red bee hums,
    The silent twilight's fall.
    Aoibheall from the Grey Rock comes
    To wrap the world in thrall.
    A *leanbhan van o*, my child, my joy,
    My love and heart's desire,
    The crickets sing you lullaby,
    Beside the dying fire.

Síobhra sails his boat till morn . . .

Rosses Point, Co. Sligo, where as a child I saw the red bees.

When I was a small child living in Sligo, my family used to go to Rosses Point during the summer months to swim. It's a small seaside place about five miles north of the town. Generally we stayed on the Near Strand, bathing and playing about on the sand, but occasionally we went over to the Far Strand. Sometimes I went off there by myself and, once or twice up by the sand banks, I noticed red bees buzzing lazily about. Whenever I mentioned them, people didn't believe me, so much so that eventually I decided I'd been mistaken and that the red bees must have been some other insect. However, they looked to me just like ordinary bees, except that they had red coats with black stripes rather than yellow coats with brown stripes. Years later, when I was eighteen and living in Dublin earning my living as a singer, I happened upon a beautiful song in the Herbert Hughes' collection of *Irish Country Songs* called 'The Gartan Mother's Lullaby'. To my surprise and great delight the opening lines were: 'Sleep, O babe, for the red bee hums the silent twilight's fall.' As Gartan is in County Donegal, a county adjacent to Sligo, I concluded that the red bee must be peculiar to the north-west coastline of Ireland. My claim to the red bees was, at last, verified.

Gartan is famous as the birthplace of Columcille (521) who gave the city of Derry its name and who is better known as the founder of a Christian outpost on the island of Iona off the west coast of Scotland. Not far away from Gartan is Rathmullin, where in 1587 young Red Hugh O'Donnell was kidnapped by a warship in disguise and brought to Dublin Castle and jail. Also from Rathmullin, the earls of Tyrone and Tyrconnell sailed into exile in 1607 leaving the way open for the plantation of Ulster, the results of which are still troubling Ireland.

The words of 'The Gartan Mother's Lullaby' are by Seosamh Mac Cathmhaoil. *Aoibheall* and *Siabhra* are fairy creatures.

She Didn't Dance

Oh she didn't dance, dance, dance,
She didn't dance at all today,
She didn't dance dance, dance,
No, nor yesterday.

CHORUS   Dance her up and up and up and up;
              And dance her up in the sky;
              Dance her up and up and up and up,
              And she 'll be down by and by.

Oh she was like a lady
She was like a queen,
She was like a lady,
Off to the fair at Glyn.

CHORUS

This is a dandling song which is sung while you bounce your baby on your knee.
I learnt it from Liam Clancy when I was living in New York City in 1956.

Tullycross, Connemara.

Anonn 's Anall

Chuirfinn mo rún go ciúin a' luascadh
'nonn 's anall
'nonn 's anall
Ar leaba bhuig chlúimh go dlú gan dúiseacht
Luascadh 'nonn 's anall;
Sláinte saol ort-sa gach oíche,
Fáilte's céad romhat-sa gach lá.
Cúmhdach Mhic De 'gus séan ort choiche,
Siúil anonn 's anall . . .

A chúilin órdha, a stór mo chroí-se,
'Nonn 's anall
'Nonn 's anall
Go stiúiri Rí na Glóire sioraí thusa
Anonn 's anall
Codhla sámh ort-sa gach oíche
Eirigh slán le Fáinne an lae.
Coinnigh do shúile dúnt' a rún dhíl
Luascadh anonn 's anall.

To and Fro

I would swing my love quietly
To and fro, to and fro
On a soft feather bed without wakening him.
Swaying to and fro,
Health and life to you each night,
A hundred and one welcomes to you each day.
May the Son of God shade you, and may you ever have luck,
Walking to and fro . . .

O golden-haired child, treasure of my heart,
Swaying to and fro, to and fro,
May the great king of eternal glory guide you to and fro
Sleep soundly each night,
Wake safely each dawn.
Keep your eyes closed, my darling,
Swaying to and fro.

My Aunt Jane

My aunt Jane, she took me in.
She gave me tea out o' her wee tin
Half a bop and a wee snow top
And cinnamon buds out o' her wee shop.

My aunt Jane has a bell at the door
A white step-stone and a clean-swept
     floor
Candy-apples and hard green pears
And conversation lozengers.

My aunt Jane can dance a jig
And sing a ballad round a sweetie pig
Wee red eyes, and a cord for a tail
Hanging in a bunch from a farthing nail.

My aunt Jane she's awful smart
She bakes a ring in an apple tart
And when that Hallow E'en comes round
Fornenst that tart I'm always found.

I first heard this song sung by Teresa Clifford when we both took part in a radio series called 'Take the Floor' on Radio Éireann. It's an Ulster children's song, a street song, evoking an innocent past for generations of youngsters. There are two kinds of children's songs – those made up for children and those made up by children themselves. The former can range from the sublime to the sickeningly sentimental; the latter have a directness and, as in 'My Aunt Jane', a surrealist imagery which is not confined by logic. As no adult can successfully paint a picture like a child, neither has an adult ever successfully captured the fragility, or indeed the harshness, of a child's spirit in song or verse.

Scorn not his Simplicity

1. See the child with the golden hair,
   Yet eyes that show the emptiness
       inside;
   Do we know, can we understand just
       how he feels?
   Or have we really tried?
   See him there as he stands alone,
   And watches children play a
       children's game.
   Simple child.
   He looks almost like the others,
   Yet they know he's not the same.
   Scorn not his simplicity
   But rather try to love him all the
       more.
   Scorn not his simplicity, oh no, oh no.

2. See him stare
   Not recognising that kind face
   That only yesterday he loved
   The loving face of a mother who can't
       understand
   What she's been guilty of.
   How she cried tears of happiness
   The day the doctor told her 'it's a
       boy'.
   Now she cries tears of helplessness
   And thinks of all the things he can't
       enjoy.
   Scorn not his simplicity
   But rather try to love him all the
       more.
   Scorn not his simplicity, oh no, oh no.

3. Only he knows
   How to face the future hopefully,
   Surrounded by despair.
   He won't ask for your pity or your
       sympathy
   But, surely, you should care?
   Scorn not his simplicity
   But rather try to love him all the
       more.
   Scorn not his simplicity, oh no, oh no.

'Scorn not his Simplicity' is one of those contemporary Irish songs that has a universal theme and appeal. It's by the Derryman, Phil Coulter, and it expresses in a compassionate and poetic way a reality in society today that is all too easily overlooked, because it makes us feel uncomfortable. The song is about a mentally-handicapped child. In the past, whenever I've sung this song in concert, parents of these children have come backstage with tears in their eyes to tell me how much they've been helped by the song. In their names I'd like to take this opportunity of saying thank you to Phil Coulter.

In Gaelic a mentally-handicapped person is often referred to as a '*duine le Dia*' or 'a person belonging to God'. This, I presume, is because of the innocence of such persons and 'Scorn not his Simplicity' conveys that sense of innocence. It also pinpoints the dilemma that their parents face.

In Derry some time ago, for a concert, I was particularly struck by the attitude of the city's community leaders toward children and young people in general. A children's music competition preceded my concert and, judging by what I could hear, the standard was high. Derry is proud of its long tradition of involvement with the arts and is determined not to let the present uncongenial political climate stunt the growth of appreciation of art among its future citizens. Kevin McCaul, one of the City Fathers in charge of the promotion of cultural activities, spoke eloquently, and indeed inspiringly, about what the city is trying to do to encourage the arts in these difficult times of civil strife in Ulster. I was very impressed with the number of eager youthful volunteers involved with organising events.

Next morning, as I toured the ancient city wall of Derry, the encouraging words of Kevin McCaul echoed in my ears, and I pondered the problems of this once beautiful city now ravaged by war. With Willie Carson, the well-known and, I might add, very patient Derry photographer at my heels, I waited for the sun to shine so we could take some photographs for this book. Brother Sun did not oblige and I had to be content with watching the River Foyle flow slowly and idly by as it has done for countless centuries into Lough Foyle.

As the day got stormier we went indoors to a reception held for me in the Mayor's office at the historic Guildhall. I signed the book and the Honourable Joe Fegan, the Mayor of the city, presented me with the city's crest, which depicts a sword, a cross, a castle and a human skeleton – a disparate looking conglomeration of emblems.

One does not normally expect to find a macabre skeleton on a city crest, and the photographer explained jokingly that it represented a passenger of the Ulster Bus waiting for a bus to return from Creggan, a one-time 'no go area' in Nationalist Derry that was fond of using buses for roadblocks. Another suggested that the skeleton represented a Derry youth waiting for a job – an appropriate enough emblem for a city that has grappled with over 40% unemployment for the past half century. However, the real story of the skeleton goes back to the early part of the seventeenth century when the planters rebuilt the city following its destruction in war. The skeleton represents a city rising out of the destruction of war; while the sword, cross and castle depict the planters' image of themselves. As if to emphasise the precarious peace that still exists in Derry, I spent most of the afternoon immobilised on a bridge that spans the River Foyle waiting for a 'loyalist' protest to run out of steam. This enforced and unexpected idleness beneath the historic walls gave me ample opportunity to watch (and contemplate) how legacies from the past can still haunt the present.

The Guildhall, the city of Derry. It is a modern gothic building completed in 1912. Among the treasures of the corporation are the Andrea Ferrara double-edged sword reputed to have belonged to Sir Cahir O'Docherty.

Déirín Dé

Déirín dé, déirín dé!
Tá'n gabhar donn ag labhairt san bhfraoch;
Déirín dé, déirín dé!
Táid na lachain ag screadaigh san bhféith.
Déirín dé, déirín dé!
Gheobhaidh basiar le heiri 'n lae
Déirín dé, déirín dé!
Is raghaidh mo leanbh da bhfeighilt ar féar.

Déirín dé, déirín dé!
Eireoidh gealach is raghaidh grian fé;
Déirín dé, déirín dé!
Is tusa mo leanbh is mo chuid den tsaol.
Déirín dé, déirín dé!
Ligfead mo leanbh ag pioca sméar;
Déirín dé, déirín dé!
Ach codladh go samh go fáinne'n lae.

The snipe is calling in the heather,
The ducks are quacking in the bog,
The cows will go west at dawn
And my child will mind them in the meadow.

The moon will rise and the sun will set.
You are my child and my share of the world.
I shall let my child gather berries
On condition that he sleeps soundly until dawn.

An Peata Circe

1. 'San -gu-gu-gu -gu -gu- gar- gair-lin,
   An-san-san-san-san-san- d'fág-as e;
   Nil bróg ar mo chois agus nil cóta 'r mo
     chorp, agus
   An gu-gu-gu-gu-gu-gar- gáir-lín.

2. Ós a tiuc-tiuc-tiuc-tiuc táim cráite 'gat,
   An culaith chuir Dia umat — bi sásta leis,
   Dá mbeadh bróg ar do chois agat is cóta'r
     do chorp, airiu!
   Bheadh cearca na dúithche ag gáiri 'mat.

3. Is ná tug-tug-tugaimse min is gráinne
     dhuit
   Is tugaim braon bainne 'gus práta dhuit
   Istoiche's tú istigh is tú ad lui ar shop t'rim
   Agus am dhóighse nil aon chuis ghearáin
     agat.

4. 'S an gu-gu-gu-gu-gu- gargáirlin,
   Bionn mo chosa gach lá san láib agam.
   Mo dhrom a bhionn fliuch is muna
     bhfóirir 'rm anois
   Ní bhéar-bhéar-bhéarfadsa ubh amáireach
     duit.

The Pet Hen

(This song starts with the clucking sound of a hen after she has laid an egg.)

1. It is over there I left it.
   I have no shoes on my feet, nor coat on my back.

2. I'm moithered with you, hen;
   The suit that God made for you, be satisfied with it.
   If you had shoes on your feet and a coat on your back,
   All the hens of the district would be laughing at you.

3. And do I not give flakes and grain to you?
   And I also give you milk and potatoes.
   And at night when you are in you lie on dry straw.
   In my opinion you have no cause for complaint.

4. My feet are every day in the mud;
   My back gets wet and if you refuse to help me now
   I won't lay an egg for you tomorrow.

The theme of the songs in this section has been, broadly speaking, children. In the next section the theme is 'fair day and market' – or so it appears on the surface. The truth is that poets and song-writers used 'fair days and markets' as pegs on which to hang their love songs.

Chapter V

She Moved Through the Fair

My young love said to me, 'My mother won't mind,
And my father won't slight you for your lack of kind.'
And she stepped away from me and this she did say,
'It will not be long, love, till our wedding day.'

She stepped away from me and she moved thro' the fair,
And fondly I watched her move here and move there;
And then she went homeward with one star awake,
As the swan in the evening moves over the lake.

Last night she came to me, my dead love came in,
So softly she came that her feet made no din;
And she laid her hand on me and this she did say,
'It will not be long, love, till our wedding day.'

'She Moved Through The Fair' can be found in authentic versions all over Ireland; three notable versions have come to light in recent times: 'In and Out The Window', 'I Once Had a True Love', and 'My Own Rod's the Sorest'. The latter was first published in the Journal of the old London-based Irish Folk Song Society, in 1905, and it was this set of words which Padraic Colum turned into 'She Moved Through the Fair'.

The song hasn't all that much to do with fairs. It belongs to a genre known as 'night-visiting songs' of which there is a great abundance in the traditions of these islands. In these songs, a parting couple make a pact that, should misfortune (death) befall either one, the departed one will return to the other. This is what happens. The girl has died (in most songs it's the boy who dies, often drowned at sea, for he appears 'cold and wet through to the skin'); she returns, and a further pact is made that 'it will not be long till our wedding day' – meaning that the bereaved is soon to follow.

As a child growing up in Ireland, the nearest I ever got to a market or fair was seeing them through the window of a car as my father slowly wove his way with difficulty through the main street of some provincial town. The way seemed jammed with a variety of livestock jostling with one another and with their owners and if, as often happened, the car window was down it was not exactly the fragrance of the cedars of Lebanon that wafted towards us. Noisy and full of life, the fairs seemed to have a decidedly festive air about them, perhaps even a sense of occasion. It is not surprising then that all the songs I know about such happenings, with the exception of 'She Moved Through the Fair', are jaunty and lighthearted.

The cattle marts and supermarkets of today, obsessed with order and clinical neatness, have superseded those colourful events. Fairs and markets provided an opportunity for people to meet socially as well as on business. They worked hard on the land for weeks on end, travel was slow and laborious and therefore time consuming and going to the market was as much an outing for them as a chance to strike a hard bargain. Fairs and markets suited a rural-based society more than an urban one. They brought variety and novelty to people's lives, giving them a chance to meet strangers.

At these gatherings there was no lack of entertainment. Dancers, musicians, ballad singers, conjurors, stunt men and all sorts of con men and women assembled together vieing with one another for the attention of the gathered crowds. Bargaining, as the songs show, was not restricted to livestock and farm produce. Many a match was made over a few pints. Among the younger folk, friendships were fostered and love bourgeoned. Indeed, as we gather from such songs as 'The Next Market Day' (p. 128) and 'Kitty of Coleraine', romance stepped in even on the way to the fair, thus preventing at least two young women from ever reaching their destination. An amorous thread runs through all songs dealing with fair days and markets.

The Next Market Day

A maid goin' to Comber, her markets to larn,
To sell for her mammy three hanks o' fine yarn,
She met with a young man along the highway,
Which caused this young damsel to dally and stray.

CHORUS   Sit ye beside me, I mean ye no harm,
Sit ye beside me this new tune to larn,
Here is three guineas your mammy to pay,
So lay by your yarn till the next market day.

They sat down together, the grass it was green,
And the day was the fairest that ever was seen,
Oh, the look in your eye beats a mornin' o' May,
I could sit by your side till the next market day.

CHORUS

This young maid went home and the words that he said
And the air that he played her still rang in her head;
She says I'll go find him by land or by sea,
Till he larns me that tune called The Next Market Day.

Sometimes 'The Next Market Day' is called 'The Comber Ballad', though it was Herbert Hughes who deliberately introduced the name 'Comber' into the song. Originally the song began 'A maid going to Erin . . .' This is one of the many songs Hughes learned from his old nurse, Ellen Boylan.

Trottin' to the Fair

Trottin' to the fair
Me and Moll Maloney,
Seated I declare,
On a single pony.

How am I to know that
Molly's safe behind,
With our heads in
Oh, that awkward, awkward way inclined.

By her gentle breathing
Whispered past my ear
And her white arms wreathin'
Warm around me here.

Thus on Dobbin's back
I discoursed the darling
Till up on the track
Leaped a mongrel snarling.

'Ah,' says Moll, 'I'm frightened, frightened,
That the pony'll start.'
And her pretty hands she tightened
Round my happy heart.

Till I axed her, 'May I
Steal a kiss or so?'
And my Molly's grey eye
Didn't answer no . . .

The words of 'Trottin' to the Fair' are by Arthur Percival Graves. Charles Villiers Stanford based his arrangement of the music on an old Irish melody.

'I'm trotting to the fair too'.

Beidh Aonach Amáireach

1. *Tá iníon agam agus tá sí óg*
Tá iníon agam agus tá sí óg
Tá iníon agam agus tá sí óg
Is tá sí i ngrá lé gréasai bróg.
Is a mháithrín a' ligfidh tú chun an aonaigh mé?
Is a mháithrín a' ligfidh tú chun an aonaigh mé?
Is a mháithrín a' ligfidh tú chun an aonaigh mé?
Is a mhúirnín ó, ná h-eití mé.

2. *Beidh aonach amáireach i gCondae an Chláir*
Beidh aonach amáireach i gCondae an Chláir
Beidh aonach amáireach i gCondae an Chláir
Cé'n mhaith dhom é, ní bheidh mé ann.
Is a mháithrín a' ligfidh tú chun an aonaigh mé?
Is a mháithrín a' ligfidh tú chun an aonaigh mé?
Is a mháithrín a' ligfidh tú chun an aonaigh mé?
Is a mhúirnín ó, ná h-eití mé.

3. *Táim-se i ngrá lé gréasaí bróg*
Táim-se i ngrá lé gréasaí bróg
Táim-se i ngrá lé gréasaí bróg
Is muna bhfaigh mé é, ní bheidh mé beó.
Is a mháithrín a' ligfidh tú chun an aonaigh mé?
'Go deimhin ní ligfead chun an aonaigh thú.'
Is a mháithrín a' ligfidh tú chun an aonaigh mé?
Is a mhúirnín ó, ná h-eití mé.

4. *Bhfearr liom féin mo ghréasai bróg*
Bhfearr liom féin mo ghréasai bróg
Bhfearr liom féin mo ghréasai bróg
Ná oifigeach airm fé na lásaí óir.
Is a mháithrín a' ligfidh tú chun an aonaigh mé?
Is a mháithrín a' ligfidh tú chun an aonaigh mé?
Is a mháithrín a' ligfidh tú chun an aonaigh mé?
Is a mhúirnín ó, ná h-eití mé.

5. *Níl tú ach a deich nó a h-aondéag fós,*
Níl tú ach a deich nó a h-aondéag fós,
Níl tú ach a deich nó a h-aondéag fós,
Nuair a bheidh tú trídéag, beidh tu mór.
Is a mháithrín a' ligfidh tú chun an aonaigh mé?
Is a mháithrín a' ligfidh tú chun an aonaigh mé?
Is a mháithrín a' ligfidh tú chun an aonaigh mé?
Is a mhúirnín ó, ná h-eití mé.

There Will be a Fair Tomorrow

1. I have a daughter and she is young,
I have a daughter and she is young,
I have a daughter and she is young,
And she's in love with a shoemaker.
Mother, won't you let me go to the fair?
Mother, won't you let me go to the fair?
Mother, won't you let me go to the fair?
Mother dear, do not refuse me.

2. There is a fair tomorrow in County Clare
There is a fair tomorrow in County Clare
There is a fair tomorrow in County Clare
What use is it to me, for I won't be there.
Mother, won't you let me go to the fair?
Mother, won't you let me go to the fair?
Mother, won't you let me go to the fair?
Mother dear, do not refuse me.

3.   I'm in love with a shoemaker,
     I'm in love with a shoemaker,
     I'm in love with a shoemaker,
     And if I don't get him I will not live.
     Mother, won't you let me go to the fair?
     Indeed I won't let you go to the fair.
     Mother, won't you let me go to the fair?
     Mother dear, do not refuse me.

4.   I would prefer my shoemaker
     I would prefer my shoemaker
     I would prefer my shoemaker
     To an army officer with gold braids.
     Mother, won't you let me go to the fair?
     Mother, won't you let me go to the fair?
     Mother, won't you let me go to the fair?
     Mother dear, do not refuse me.

5.   You're not ten or eleven yet
     You're not ten or eleven yet
     You're not ten or eleven yet
     When you are thirteen you'll be grown up.
     Mother, won't you let me go to the fair?
     Mother, won't you let me go to the fair?
     Mother, won't you let me go to the fair?
     Mother dear, do not refuse me.

Sligo Fair

1. I have a bonnet trimmed with blue
Shoes with bows and stockings new,
Ribbons blue will tie my hair
When I go to Sligo Fair.

2. In my bonnet trim'd with blue,
Do you like me? yes you do.
I will wear it when I can,
Going to the fair with my young man.

3. I have a bonnet trimmed with blue,
Do I wear it? yes, I do.
I will wear it when I can,
Going to the fair with my o young man.

4. My young man has gone to sea;
When he comes home he'll play for me.
Tip to the heel and tip to the toe,
That's the way the polkie goes.

5. I have a bonnet trimmed with blue,
Do I wear it? yes I do.
I will wear it when I can,
Going to the fair with my young man.

'Sligo Fair' is an adapted version of the song, 'I have a Bonnet Trimmed With Blue'. The origin of this song is uncertain. The polka rhythm and the original words, 'going to the ball with my young man', as opposed to 'going to the fair' as I sing it, suggests that the song probably came from England. I learnt this song as a young girl at St Anne's private junior school, which was attached to the Ursuline convent in Sligo. Jill Noone, an interesting and lettered woman, taught it to our class as an action song. She also took us for games, drill, elocution and choral recitation.

In bygone days, fairs and markets played an essential role in the economic and social life of Ireland. The songs reflect something of the high jinks that were associated with 'going off to the fair'. Some of the songs in the next chapter would undoubtedly have been aired at many a fair. The Spanish Lady and her festive, if rather eccentric behaviour, sets the tone for what I call humorous Songs of Ireland.

Chapter VI

The Spanish Lady

As I walked down through Dublin city,
At the hour of twelve of the night,
Who should I spy but a Spanish lady,
Washing her feet by candle light.
First she washed them,
Then she dried them,
O'er a fire of amber coal.
In all my life, I ne'er did see,
A maid so neat about the sole.

CHORUS   Whack for the too–ra loo–ra lady
               Whack for the too–ra loo–ra lee
               Whack for the too–ra loo–ra lady
               Whack for the too–ra loo–ra lee

As I came through Dublin city,
At the hour of half–past eight,
Who should I spy but a Spanish lady
Brushing her hair in broad daylight.
First she tossed it, then she brushed it,
On her lap was a silver comb,
In all my life I ne'er did see,
So fair a maid since I did roam.

CHORUS

As I went down through Dublin city
When the sun began to set,
Who should I spy but a Spanish lady,
Catching a moth in a golden net.
When she saw me, then she fled me,
Lifting her petticoat over the knee,
In all my life I ne'er did see,
A maid so blithe as the Spanish lady.

CHORUS

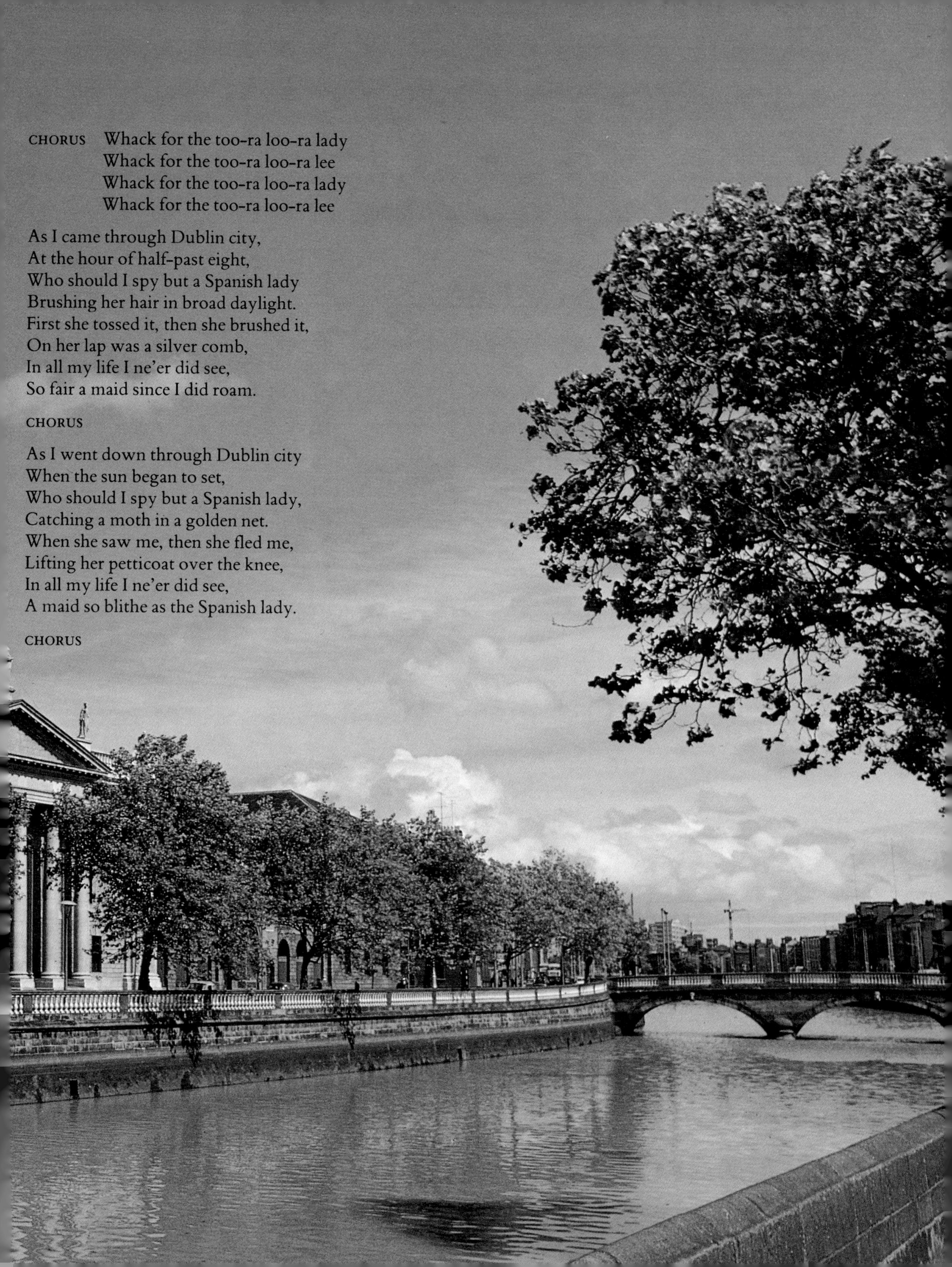

Merrion Square, a good example of Georgian architecture in Dublin.

At least one authority on Irish vocal music has claimed that women singers in Gaelic Ireland never sang humorous songs because such songs were supposed to detract from their dignity. If humour is taken to mean crudeness, then I wholly agree. However, in my opinion, a well-balanced programme of songs requires a mixture of the serious and the light-hearted. The Irish tradition has many examples of both categories, and 'The Spanish Lady' exemplifies the latter.

I heard 'The Spanish Lady' for the first time many years ago in Dublin. The singer was Tom Kinsella; the occasion, a party in his flat in Baggot Street off Saint Stephen's Green. Tom, who was even then a well-known literary figure, but whose poetry has since been internationally acclaimed, introduced me to my future husband, Richard Selig. Another version of this song, delightful not least because of its images of the unexpected, has the singer walking down through Galway city instead of Dublin. It doesn't much matter which city is the setting for this light-hearted and amusing account of the eccentric behaviour of the Spanish Lady. It is one of the earliest songs added to my repertoire after I left school and was one of the four I chose for the test recording I made for the Decca Recording Company at the start of my career.

Ceól a' Píobaire

1. Má phósann tú an sistealóir, 's tú bhéas a'
    caoine,
    'S a mhúrnín dílis 's fhaoileann ó!
    Beidh tú i do thachta lé barrach na tíre,
    'S a mhúirnín dílis 's fhaoileann ó!
    Ó beidh tú i do shuí go mbeidh sé an
        mhean oiche,
    A' sior-dhó na gcoinneal 's a' sgioba an lín
        dó,
    Ach ba mhíle fearr dhuit mise 'gat is ceól
        binn mo phíobaí
    'S a mhúirnín dílis is fhaoileann ó!

2. Má phósann tú an figheadóir is tú bhéas a
    caoine,
    'S a mhúirnín dílis is fhaoileann ó!
    Beidh céad luig-laig ag an ugham dá
        sgaoileadh,
    'S a mhúirnín dílis is fhaoileann ó!
    Ó beidh tú i do shuí go mbeidh sé an
        mhean oiche,

    A sior- dhó na gcoinneal 's a' crónán
        faoi'n ineadh,
    Ach ba mhíle fearr dhuit mise 'gat is ceól
        binn mo phíobaí,
    'S a mhúirnín dílis is fhaoileann ó!

3. Má phósann tú an t-oibri, is tú bhéas go
        h-aoibhinn,
    'S a mhúirnín dílis is fhaoileann ó!
    Gheóbhadh tú marcaíocht chun an
        aonaigh,
    'S a mhúirnín dílis is fhaoileann ó!
    Ní bheidh tú i do shuí go mbeidh sé an
        mhean oiche,
    Beidh airgead i do phócai 's ór buí ina
        phíosaí,
    Ach, ba mhíle fearr dhuit mise 'gat is ceól
        binn mo phíobaí,
    'S a mhúirnín dílis is fhaoileann ó!

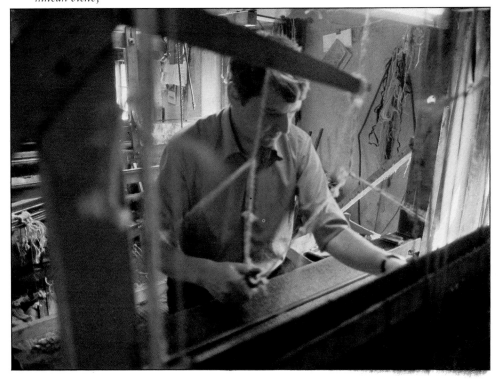

The Music of the Piper

If you marry the flax gatherer, 'tis you who'll be sorry,
O my love and my darling,
You'll be choked with the chaff of the land
O my love and my darling.
You'll be up till midnight
For ever burning candles and handing him the linen.
But you'd be better off with me and the sweet music of my pipes
O my love and my darling.

If you marry the weaver, 'tis you who'll be sorry,
O my love and my darling,
You'll be hearing the monotonous shuttling of the loom
O my love and my darling.
You'll be up till midnight
For ever burning candles and muttering about thread.
But you'd be better off with me and the sweet music of my pipes
O my love and my darling.

If you marry the worker, 'tis you who'll be doing nicely,
O my love and my darling,
You'll get a ride to the market,
O my love and my darling.
You'll not be awake till midnight
And you'll have silver in your pockets and pieces of gold
But you'd be better off with me and the sweet music of my pipes
O my love and my darling.

The young man in 'The Music of The Piper' ('*Ceól a'Phiobaire*') is blest with a superabundance of self confidence. One gets the impression that he hasn't a penny to his name and, apart from making music, is probably unemployed. He tells the girl he loves that it's a complete waste of her time considering marrying any of her other suitors: some of them have nothing to recommend them, and, the one who has – sure, he's not a patch on himself and the sweet music of his pipes. The hero of this song has many silver-tongued parallels in Irish song and literature, most notably in Synge's *In the Shadow of the Glen*, in which a traveller pours most extravagant blandishments on a poor girl, describing to her life on the road under the stars, leaving her troubles and hardships behind. He doesn't have a penny to his name either, but his speech is beyond price.

The Stuttering Lovers

1. A wee bit over the lee me lads
   A wee bit over the lee;
   The birds went into the poor man's
      corn,
   I fear they'll never be s-s-s-s-seen me
      lads
   I fear they'll never be seen.

2. Then out comes the bonny wee lass
   And she was one so fair,
   And she went into the poor man's
      corn,
   To see if the birds were
      th-th-th-th-there me lads
   To see if the birds were there.

3. Then out comes the bonny wee lad,
   And he was a fisherman's son.
   And he went into the poor man's
      corn,
   To see if the lass was th-th-th-th-there
      me lads,
   To see if the lass was there.

4. He kissed her once and he kissed her
      twice,
   He kissed her ten times over,
   Oh it's nice to be kissing the bonny
      wee lass,
   That's never been kissed
      bef-f-f-f-fore me lads,
   That's never been kissed before.

5. Then out comes the poor old man
   And he was tattered and torn;
   'If that's the way you're minding the
      birds,
   I'll mind them meself in the
      m-m-m-m-m-morn me lad,
   I'll mind them meself in the morn.'

'The Stuttering Lovers' was the first song ever taken down from a traditional singer by Herbert Hughes. He found it near Letterkenny in County Donegal, eighty years ago. Hughes had gone to Donegal at the insistence of his mentor Francis Joseph Bigger, antiquarian, historian, and a host of other things, who had urged the youthful musician to betake himself to this remote corner of Ireland and listen to the songs being sung by the common people there.

Getting into darkest Donegal in those days was no easy matter. A contemporary traveller has left us a vivid description:

> After travelling over roads almost impassable, over hills almost
> inaccessible, every ligature and joint in my poor body was nearly jolted
> into dislocation . . .

Hughes met the master of the workhouse at Dunfanaghy, a bleak little town on the very edge of the north Atlantic Ocean, and through him came to meet some of the inmates from the workhouse, or 'union' as they were sometimes called, and some other local musicians. What Hughes heard from their lips and from their tattered fiddles was to change his whole course in life from classical composer to folksong arranger. 'The Stuttering Lovers' is the first song in his first notebook. From this stemmed the masterwork he called *Irish Country Songs*, and which took him twenty-seven years to complete, the fourth volume of which was published just the year before he died.

Sean 'Sa Bhriste Leathair

1. *Nuair a bhíos i dtúis mo shaoil,*
   'S mé ag eirí suas im' leanbh
   Bhí orm greann gach aoinne
   Ba mise peata an cheana.
   Nuair a bhíos ag dul 'sna déagaibh
   Do théighinn i measc na bhfearaibh
   Níor mhór dom féin 'na dhéidh sin
   Iompáil amach am' ghaige.

   CHORUS   *Ri-too-ra-lu-ra-la*
   Ri-to-ra-lu-r-laddie.
   Ri-too-ra-lu-ra-la
   Sean 'sa bhriste leathair

2. *Bhi orm culaith dheas éadai*
   I n-iúl do rí nó marcuis,
   Casóigín deas bréide
   Is bheistin glégeal flannel.
   Stocaí de ghlas caorach
   'Gus bróigín Gaelach smeartha
   Hata íseal Quaker
   Agus sceilp de bhriste leathair.

   CHORUS

3. The piper to help sport
   He played some tunes so jolly
   Faith he played some charming notes
   To banish melancholy.
   When he put on the pipes
   He played 'Sweet Highland Mary'
   Oh you'd laugh until you'd cry
   Just to hear poor Paddy Carey

   CHORUS

Sean and his Leather Breeches

In the early part of my life
When I was growing up as a child,
I was everybody's pet.
In my teens,
I moved among the men
And turned into a real dandy.

CHORUS   Ri-too-ra-lu-ra-la,
Sean and his leather breeches.

I wore a suit of clothes
Fit for king or marquis,
A neat tweed jacket
And a vest made of flannel;
Stockings of grey wool
With glossy Irish shoes,
A flat Quaker hat
And tight leather breeches.

CHORUS

According to Seán Óg, the words of this song are not all that old – probably
dating from the middle of the last century – but the air is traditional and therefore
much older. It is actually a dance-tune and was used for *portaireach rinnce*, that is,
dance-lilting, when no musical instrument was available. The rhythm is that of
the reel.

The Frog's Wedding

1. There was a frog lived in the well,
     hi! ho! said Roly.
   There was a frog lived in the well,
     and a merry mouse in the dell.
   With me Roly, poly, cabbage, and
     spinach, and hi! for Anthony
     Roly

2. Said the frog, I must go court, hi! ho!
     said Roly.
   Said the frog, I must go court, with
     my bayonet and my sword;
   With me Roly poly, cabbage and
     spinach, and hi! for Anthony
     Roly.

3. Where will the wedding be? hi! ho!
     said Roly.
   Where will the wedding be?
   Down at the butt of an ivy tree,
   With me Roly poly cabbage and
     spinach and hi! for Anthony
     Roly.

4. Now we're all in very good cheer,
     hi! ho! said Roly.
   Now we're all in very good cheer,
   If we had some music here,
   With me Roly, poly, cabbage, and
     spinach, and hi! for Anthony
     Roly.

5. In came the bumble bee, hi! ho! said
     Roly.
   In came the bumble bee
   Clapped a bagpipe on his knee,
   With me Roly, poly, cabbage, and
     spinach, and hi! for Anthony
     Roly.

6. Now we're all in very good cheer,
     hi! ho! said Roly.
   Now we're all in very good cheer
   If we had some dancing here,
   With me Roly poly, cabbage and
     spinach, and hi! for Anthony
     Roly.

7. In came the butterfly, hi! ho! said
     Roly.
   In came the butterfly
   Swore to dance until she'd die,
   With me Roly, poly, cabbage, and
     spinach, and hi! for Anthony
     Roly.

8. Then commenced a terrible din, hi!
     ho! said Roly.
   Then commenced a terrible din
   The cat and her kittens came
     tumbling in,
   With me Roly, poly, cabbage, and
     spinach, and hi! for Anthony
     Roly.

9. The cat took poor mister rat by the
     head, hi! ho! said Roly.
   The cat took poor mister rat by the
     head,
   And the kittens killed poor miss
     mousie dead,
   With me Roly, poly, cabbage, and
     spinach, and hi! for Anthony
     Roly.

10. Frog jumped up with a terrible
     fright, hi! ho! said Roly.
   Frog jumped up with a terrible fright
   Doffed his hat and said 'good-night',
   With me Roly, poly, cabbage, and
     spinach, and hi! for Anthony
     Roly.

11.   As the frog was crossing the stream,
          hi! ho! said Roly.
      As the frog was crossing the stream,
      A big duck came and gobobbld him
          up,
      With me Roly, poly, cabbage, and
          spinach, and hi! for Anthony
          Roly.

'The Frog's Wedding' is a good example of a song of which different versions are found elsewhere in the English-speaking world. Most people will know the Burl Ives American version: 'A Frog Went a-Courting' but I learnt this Irish version from Liam Clancy.

In the mid-seventies I gave a series of recitals in schools throughout Ireland under the auspices of the Music Association of Ireland. 'The Frog's Wedding' was always a particular success with the children. One function of these mini recitals was to explain the versatility of the harp, an instrument especially effective for simulating the drone-like sound of the bumble bee, the sound of the bagpipes and for illustrating the delicate dance of the butterfly. Before starting the series, I wanted to test how children would react to my programme and so I tried it out on a captive audience of four, the children of my great friend Déirdre Kelleher in Dublin. After explaining to my audience that the 'Frog's Wedding' was about a dramatically short and a very mixed marriage, with both bride and groom meeting with disaster on their wedding day, little eight-year old Ruth looked up at me with a tearful expression and said: 'Oh, Mary, they were never meant for each other.'

So-called 'nonsense' songs such as this sometimes have profound undertones. Animals performing the functions of humans has been a ploy for some serious satires on human behaviour. There are fox-hunting songs in which the fox leaves a will bequeathing his brush and cap to the master of the hounds. In 'Larry's Goat', the goat, about to be slaughtered because he ate some garden greens, bequeaths even his bones, teeth, and beard to the odious collection of villagers who have been tormenting him all his life.

Kitty of Coleraine

As beautiful Kitty one morning was tripping,
With a pitcher of milk from the fair of Coleraine,
When she saw him she stumbled, the pitcher it tumbled
And all the sweet buttermilk watered the plain.
Oh! what shall I do now, 'twas looking at you now,
Sure, sure, such a pitcher I'll ne'er meet again.
'Twas the pride of my dairy, oh Barney McCleary,
You're sent as a plague on the girls of Coleraine.

He sat down beside her and gently did chide her,
That such a misfortune, should give her such pain.
A kiss then he gave her, and before he did leave her,
She vowed for such pleasure, she'd break it again.
'Twas haymaking season, I can't tell the reason,
Misfortune will never come single 'tis plain.
For very soon after poor Kitty's disaster,
The divil a pitcher was whole in Coleraine.

'Kitty of Coleraine' is a song from County Derry in Northern Ireland. As the song shows, Kitty was not one to miss a good opportunity. She was quick to turn a mishap to her advantage, proving, if such were needed, that there are occasions when it pays off to cry over spilt milk. Furthermore, it looks as though her serendipitous discovery started a trend in Coleraine which left the town not only without pitchers, but probably without unattached young ladies as well.

Like death and the taxman, sorrow is unavoidable in the lives of all of us.

> 'Plaisir d'amour ne dure que moment
> Chagrin d'amour dure toute la vie . . .'

This sentiment expressed in the well-known seventeenth-century French song sums up the theme of the next chapter.

OPPOSITE *Haymaking. 'Twas the haymaking season, I can't tell the reason . . . .'*

Chapter VII

The Last Rose of Summer

1. 'Tis the last rose of summer
Left blooming alone;
All her lovely companions
Are faded and gone;
No flower of her kindred,
No rose-bud is nigh,
To reflect back her blushes,
Or give sigh for sigh.

2. I'll not leave thee, thou lone one!
To pine on the stem;
Since the lovely are sleeping,
Go to sleep thou with them.
Thus kindly I scatter
Thy leaves o'er the bed,
Where thy mates of the garden
Lie scentless and dead.

3. So soon may I follow,
When friendships decay,
And from Love's shining circle
The gems drop away.
When true hearts lie wither'd
And fond ones are flown,
Oh! who would inhabit
This bleak world alone?

'The Last Rose of Summer', another of Thomas Moore's songs, is as well-known internationally as the 'Londonderry Air'. Like so many of Moore's compositions, the melody is much older than the words. In 1834 Moore had published the last of his *Irish Melodies*. Shortly before that, he had published a *History of Ireland*, *Travels of an Irishman in Search of Religion*, and *The Life of Lord Edward Fitzgerald*. After all those, 'The Last Rose of Summer' could well be the final statement of a disillusioned and weary poet but the sad fact is, that for a number of years before he died, Moore became prematurely senile and indeed did 'inhabit this bleak world alone'. Perhaps in writing 'The Last Rose of Summer' he had a premonition about his own eventual mental isolation from friends and family to be 'left blooming alone'.

Much has been said about Moore's embezzlement of Bunting's musical funds, even though Bunting himself took some liberties with the music of the harpers at the Belfast Harp Festival. If Bunting resented Moore's successes as a songwriter, especially when Moore had helped himself from Bunting's collection in his search for melodies, then he must have had some recompense in seeing Moore in his own turn plagiarised by the German composer, Friedrich von Flotow who, in his opera *Marta*, gave 'The Last Rose of Summer', complete and with no credits, to the soprano as one of her arias.

Bríd Óg Ní Mháille
(Young Bridget O'Malley)

1. Oh! *Bríd Óg Ní Mháille*, 'tis you've
   left my heart shaken
   With a hopeless desolation, so before
   you I stand;
   Oh! 'tis wonders of admiration, your
   quiet face has taken,
   And your beauty would awaken the
   ones of the Golden Land.

2. Oh! the white moon above the pale
   sands and the pale stars upon the
   thorn tree,
   Are cold beside my darling, but no
   purer than she;
   Oh I gaze upon the cold moon till the
   stars drown in the warm sea
   But the bright eyes of my darling are
   never on me.

3. The Sunday is weary, the Sunday is
   grey now;
   My heart is a cold thing, my heart is a
   stone.
   All joy is dead in me, my life's gone
   away now,
   Another has taken my love for his
   own.

The version above of '*Bríd Óg Ní Mháille*' ('Young Bridget O'Malley') is a translation by my sister Joan. I sing the song both in the original Gaelic and in English.

Cá Rabhais Ar Fea An Lae Uaim

1. *Cá raibhis ar fea an lae uaim, a*
   bhuachailín ó?
   Cá rabhais are fea an lae uaim, a lao dhil
   'sa stór?
   Ag fiach 'sa foghlaereacht, a mháithrín ó!
   'Gus cóirigh mo leaba, táim breóite go
   leór.

2. *Cad d'ithis dod dhínnéar, a bhuachaillin*
   ó?
   Cad d'ithis dod dhínnéar, a lao dhil 's
   stór?
   D'itheas sicíní nimhe ar phláitíní óir
   Is cóirigh mo leaba, táim breóite go leór.

3. *Cad fhágfair aged' athair, a bhuachaillin*
   ó?
   Cad fhágfair aged' athair, a lao dhil 's
   stór?
   Cóiste 's cheithre capaill, a mháithrín ó!
   Is cóirigh mo leaba, táim breóite go leór.

4. *Cad fhágfair aged' mháthair, a*
   bhuachaillin ó?
   Cad a fhágfair aged' mháthair, a lao dhil
   's stór?
   Mo bha 's mo chuid tailimh, a mháithrín
   ó!
   Is cóirigh mo leaba, táim breóite go leór.

5. *Cad fhágfair aged' mhnaoi phósta, a*
   bhuachaillin ó?
   Cad fhágfair aged' mhnaoi phósta, a lao
   dhil 's stór?
   Croch chun a chrochta is téad láidir, a
   máithrín ó!
   Is cóirigh mo leaba, táim breóite go leór.

Lord Randall

1. Where were you all day, O my young
   man,
   Where were you all day, O my
   darling?
   Hunting and shooting, O mother
   dear,
   And get my bed ready, for I'm
   desperately sick.

2. What had you for dinner, O my
   young man?
   What had you for dinner, O my
   darling?
   I had poisoned chicken on a golden
   plate,
   And get my bed ready, for I'm
   desperately sick.

3. What shall you bequeath your father,
   O my young man?
   What shall you bequeath your father,
   O my darling?
   A coach with four horses, O mother
   dear,
   And get my bed ready, for I'm
   desperately sick.

4. What shall you bequeath your
   mother, O my young man?
   What shall you bequeath your
   mother, O my darling?
   My land and my cattle, O mother
   dear,
   And get my bed ready, for I'm
   desperately sick.

5. What shall you bequeath your wife,
   O my young man?
   What shall you bequeath your wife, O
   my darling?
   A gibbet for to hang her and a strong
   rope, O mother dear,
   And get my bed ready, for I'm
   desperately sick.

6. *Cár mhaith leat bheith curtha, a bhuachaillin ó?*
   Cár mhaith leat bheith curtha, a lao dhil 's a stór?
   I dTeampall Chill Mhuire, a mháithrin ó!
   Is cóirigh mo leaba, táim breóite go leór.

6. Where would you like to be buried, O my young man?
   Where would you like to be buried, O my darling?
   In the churchyard of Cill Muire, O mother dear,
   And get my bed ready, for I'm desperately sick.

'*Cá Rabhais Ar Fea An Lae Uaim*' is a Gaelic version of the well-known song 'Lord Randall', sung for centuries throughout Europe. The original Lord Randall may be any one of the three notorious twelfth-century Earls of Chester. Two of them were named Randal and all of them were involved in poisoning incidents. The song's perennial attraction may be due to its universal theme (the jealous sweetheart, the return to the mother, bequests of considerable property) and to the easily memorized story told in dialogue form. There are English, Lowland Scots and American versions of this song – all sung to different melodies – and in America alone the hero has twenty-eight different names. In the Irish version the lethal dish was 'chicken on a golden plate', but elsewhere it was 'eels boiled in broth'.

The Irish seem to have a particular aversion to fish – an aversion not unconnected, perhaps, with eating fish on a Friday – and a dish of eels would not be regarded as a particularly enticing form of bait for a young man, even if it was served on a golden plate. The type of plate, of course, gives the listener an indication of the affluence of the people involved, just as the rich bequests do. The universal popularity of this song seems to indicate that the doings of the rich was always a favourite curiosity of the poor.

The Bonny Boy

The trees are growing high my love, and the grass is growing green;
And many a cold and winter night that I alone have been.
It is a cruel and bitter night that I must lie alone,
Oh! the Bonny boy is young, but he is growing

Oh! father, dear father I think you did me wrong
For to go and get me married to one that is so young.
He is but sixteen years and I am twenty-one.
Oh! the bonny boy is young and he's growing

Oh! daughter, dear daughter, I did not do you wrong
For to go and get you married to one that is so young.
He will be a match for you when I am dead and gone.
Oh! the bonny boy is young – but he's growing

Oh! father, dear father, I'll tell you what I'll do;
I'll send my love to college for another year or two;
And all around his college cap, I'll bind a ribbon blue,
For to let the ladies know that he's married.

A year it went by and I passed the college wall
And saw the young collegians a–playing at the ball;
I spied him in among them, the fairest of them all,
Oh! my bonny boy was young and still growing.

At the age of sixteen years he was a married man,
And at the age of seventeen the father of a son,
But at the age of eighteen, o'er his grave the grass grew green;
Cruel death put an end to his growing.

I'll buy my love a shroud of the Holland linen brown;
And whilst they are making it, the tears they will run down;
It's once I had a true love, but now he's lying low,
And I'll nurse his bonny boy while he's growing.

An Raibh Tú ag an gCarraig Were you at the Rock?

An raibh tú a' gCarraig, nó a'bhfaca tú féin
    mo ghrá?
Nó a' bhfaca tú gille, fine, agus scéimh na
    mná?
Nó a' bhfaca tú an t-ubhall ba chúmhra 's ba
    mhílse blá?
Nó a' bhfaca tú mo Valentine, nó a bhfuil sí'na
    claoi mar atáim?

Do bhí mé ag a' gCarraig, is do chonnaic mé
    féin do ghrá.
Is do chonnaic mé gille, fine, and agus scéimh
    na mná.
Is do chonnaic mé an t-ubhall ba chúmhra 's ba
    mhílse blá,
Is do chonnaic mé do Valentine, is níl sí 'na
    claoi mar atáir.

Nuair a luighimse am chodladh, bíonn osna
    gan bhri 'mo chleibh
Is mé am shuí idir cnocaibh go dtiocfaí an
    ghrian aniar,
A rún dhíl 's a chogaìr, níl furthacht mo chúis
    ach Dia.
Is go ndearna loch fola de sholas mo shúil id
    dhéidh.

Were you at the Rock and did you see my
    love?
Did you see her fair complexion and her
    beauty?
Or did you see the apple blossom that is
    fairest of them all?
Or did you see my Valentine or is she
    pining as I am?

I was at the Rock and I saw your love,
I saw her fair complexion and her beauty.
I saw the apple blossom that is fairest of
    them all,
And I saw your Valentine and she is not
    pining like you are.

When I lie down to sleep, there is an
    aching sigh in my breast,
And I sitting in a dark valley between hills
    until the sun rises.
My darling and my secret, only God can
    relieve my condition,
For my eyes have become lakes of blood
    because of you.

Seán Óg taught me this song and told me that Carraig referred to *Carraig an Aifrinn*, or the Mass Rock, a recognised rendezvous in penal-day Ireland. In those days, priests and the Mass were outlawed and, since the faithful were not permitted churches, they congregated secretly to attend Mass in out-of-the-way places, generally in the hills. A large rock became an altar, hence, the Mass Rock. Many such Rocks can still be seen today in isolated valleys and on wild mountainsides throughout Ireland. As in this song, it would have been perfectly normal for a man to ask a friend if he had been to Mass and seen his beloved there.

Ballinderry

1. 'Tis pretty to be in Ballinderry,
    'Tis pretty to be in Aghalee,
    'Tis prettier to be in bonny Ram's
        Island
    Trysting under an ivy tree.
    Ochone Ó! ochone! ochone! ochone!

2. Oft times I'd sail to bonny Ram's
        Island,
    Side by side with Phelim my
        diamond;
    And often he'd court me, and I'd be
        coy –
    In my heart, how I loved him, my
        darling boy.
    Ochone Ó! ochone! ochone! ochone!

3. 'I'm going,' he said, 'from bonny
        Ram's Island,
    Out and across the stormy sea,
    And if in your heart you love me,
        Mary,
    Open your arms at last to me.'
    Ochone Ó! ochone! ochone!

4. I opened my arms, ah, well he knew
        me!
    I opened my arms and took him to
        me;
    And under the shade of the moaning
        mast,
    We kissed our first and we kissed our
        last.
    Ochone Ó! ochone! ochone!

5. I wish I were the weeping willow,
   I'd wander along by the lonesome sea.
   And cry to him over the cruel sea;
   Ah, Phelim my diamond, Come
        home to me.
   Ochone Ó! ochone! ochone!

6. 'Twas pretty to be in Ballinderry,
   But now 'tis sad as sad can be;
   For the ship that sailed with Phelim
        my diamond,
   Is sunk forever beneath the sea.
   Ochone Ó! ochone! ochone!

Ballinderry is in County Antrim and Ram's Island is on Lough Neagh, the largest lake in the British Isles, extending over 153 square miles. The island is the largest on the lake and contains the ruins of an ancient round tower. Wolfe Tone with some of the northern leaders of the United Irishmen visited the island in 1795. At the outflow of the River Bann from Lough Neagh is another place also celebrated in song, Toome Bridge. The bridge spanning the river was destroyed by insurgents who tried to delay General Knox after the Battle of Antrim in 1798.

'I'd wander along by the lonesome billow And cry to him over the cruel sea'.

Caoine Chill Cais   The Lament for Cill Cais

Cad a dhéanfaimid feasta gan adhmad,
Tá deire na gcoillte ar lár,
Is gan trácht ar Chill Cais ná a teaghlach,
'Sní bhuailfear a creidhil go brá.
An áit úd 'na gcónaionn an dea-bhean,
Fuair gradam is meidhir thar mnáibh,
Bhíodh iarlaí ag tarrant thar tuinn ann,
'S an t-Aifreann binn dá rá.

Ní chluinnim fuaim lachann na géann' ann,
Ná fiolar i gcéin cois cuain,
Ná fiú na beacha chum saoithir,
Thiúrfadh mil agus ceir do'n tslua.
Níl ceól binn milis na n-ean ann,
Le hamharc an lae dul uainn,
Ná an chuaichin i mbarraibh na gcraobh ann,
Ó'sí chuirfeadh an saol chum suain.

Is aitchim ar Mhuire 's ar Íosa,
Go dtagaidh si 'ris chugainn slán,
Go mbeidh rainnce fada gabhail timcheall,
Ceól bheidhlín is teinnte cnámh.
Go dtógfar an baile seo'r sinnsear,
Cill Cais bhreá arís go hárd,
Is go brá nó go dtiocfaidh an díleann,
Ná feicfear i 'rist ar lár.

What shall we do without timber,
Now that the forests are all cut down?
It shall never be surpassed,
Cill Cais, where the good woman lived,
Praised and respected beyond all others.
Earls came there from abroad
And melodious Mass was there
    celebrated.

The sound of geese or ducks will never
    again be heard there,
Nor eagle by the bay;
No bees busily working,
Making honey and wax for the multitude.
The sweet music of birds is no longer
    there
To be heard as evening light fades,
No cuckoo in the tree-tops
To lull the world to sleep.

I implore Mary and Jesus,
That the good lady may return to us
    safely,
That once more there'll be dancing and
    merry-go-round,
The sound of the violen and bonfires.
May the seat of our ancestors be rebuilt
With far greater splendour,
And may it never again, till doomsday,
Fall into ruin.

The castle of Cill Cais, one of the chief seats of the Butler family, is situated at the foot of Sliabh na mBan, a mountain in County Tipperary that gave a title to that famous song on (p. 79). The words are attributed to a man called Lane whom Lady Iveagh (the *deá-bhean* referred to in the song) helped to educate for the priesthood. The song laments the cutting down of the forests and the passing of the old order and the melody is a very beautiful one. Every schoolboy and schoolgirl in Ireland knows this song because it is always on the Gaelic-language school syllabus and at some stage or other has to be learnt off by heart. I have been singing it since school days.

Although I was unaware of it at the time, this song played a significant role in my meeting Richard Selig, my late husband. During his first visit to Ireland he

heard me singing it on a Radio Éireann programme where I was a guest artiste with the Radio Éireann Singers. He interrupted a conversation he was having with some friends to listen until the announcer gave my name. He told me afterwards that it was the sadness in my voice that first arrested his attention. For him, a newcomer and stranger to Ireland, it seemed to confirm the truth of Chesterton's oft quoted dictum that in Ireland all their wars are merry and their songs, sad.

Down by the Sally Gardens

Down by the sally gardens,
My love and I did meet.
She passed the sally gardens,
With little snow-white feet.
She bid me take love easy,
As the leaves grow on the tree,
But I was being young and foolish,
With her did not agree.

In a field by the river,
My love and I did stand;
And on my leaning shoulder,
She placed her snow-white hand;
She bid me take life easy,
As the grass grows on the weirs,
But I was young and foolish,
And now am full of tears.

The words of 'Down By The Sally Gardens' are by W. B. Yeats; Herbert Hughes set them to the music of an old traditional air called 'The Maids of Mourne Shore'. The poem itself is from *Crossways*, a set of poems written by Yeats before he was twenty-one in about 1889. He regularly threatened to omit most of them from subsequent anthologies, relenting only (he said) because a school friend claimed that they reminded him of his childhood.

A sally is a willow tree and most towns and villages had sally gardens to provide rods for use in thatching. They also provided school teachers and disciplinarian parents with convenient sticks to beat naughty children. The sally gardens outside Sligo, the subject of this poem, have long ago disappeared giving way to a housing estate.

I Will Walk with my Love

I once loved a boy and a bold Irish boy
Who would come and would go at my request;
And this bold Irish boy was my pride and my joy,
And I built him a bower in my breast.

I once loved a boy and a bonny bonny boy,
And a boy that I thought was my own;
But he loves another far deeper than me,
And has taken his flight and is gone.

But this girl who has taken my bonny bonny boy
Let her make of him all that she can,
And whether he loves me or loves me not,
I will walk with my love now and then.

'I Will Walk with my Love' is a traditional song from County Dublin. I first recorded it in 1957 in New York City for inclusion in the album, *Love Songs of Ireland*, which was released just after my husband's death.

I Know my Love

1. I know my love by his way of
      walkin',
   And I know my love by his way of
      talkin',
   And I know my love dressed in a suit
      of blue,
   And if my love leaves me what will I
      do?

CHORUS   And still she cried, 'I love him
               the best,
            And a troubled mind, sure, can
               know no rest.'
            And still she cried, 'Bonny boys
               are few,
            And if my love leaves me, what
               will I do?'

2. There is a dance house in Maradyke,
   And there my true love goes ev'ry
      night,
   He takes a strange one on his knee,
   And don't you think now that vexes
      me?

CHORUS

3. If my love knew I could wash and
      wring,
   If my love knew I could weave and
      spin,
   I'd make a coat all of the finest kind,
   But the want of money, sure, leaves
      me behind.

CHORUS

4. I know my love is an arrant rover,
   I know he'll wander the wide world
      over;
   In dear old Ireland he'll no longer
      tarry,
   And a foreign one he is sure to marry.

CHORUS

5. Oh! I'll not fret and I'll not be pining,
   And so my beauty won't be declining;
   I'll just let on that I don't care a pin,
   And sure that's the best way his heart
      to win.

CHORUS

The Parting

When my love and I parted, the wind blew cold,
When my love and I parted our love untold
How my heart kept crying: 'love come with me,'
But he turned his face from me and sought the sea.

When my love and I parted we shed no tears.
Though we knew that between us lay weary years;
And a bird was singing upon a tree
And a gleam of sunlight lay on the sea.

Parting is bitter and weeping vain
And all true lovers will meet again
And no fate can sever my love from me
For his heart is the river and mine the sea.

In joy and in sorrow, Nature provides the poet with ready images for clothing his sentiments. In the next chapter, the songs are chiefly concerned with nature and outdoor life. In our part of the world it is rare indeed to find a song lauding a wet day, but that is what the song heading the next chapter in fact does.

Chapter VIII

A Soft Day

A soft day, thank God!
A wind from the south
With a honey'd mouth,
A scent of drenching leaves,
Briar and beech and lime,
White elder-flower and thyme
And the soaking grass smells sweet,
Crushed by my two bare feet,
While the rain drips, drips, drips from the
    eaves.

A soft day, thank God!
The hills wear a shroud of silver cloud;
The web the spider weaves is a glittering
    net;
The woodland path is wet,
And the soaking earth smells sweet
Under my two bare feet,
And the rain drips, drips, drips, drips
    from the leaves.

The words of 'A Soft Day' are by W. M. Letts and the music is by C. V. Stanford. Whenever I have stayed in the Aran Islands, I couldn't help noticing what a significant part the weather played in the lives of the people. First thing in the morning, the man of the house would stick his head out the door 'to look at the weather' and then deliver his judgement about the coming day. He would even give the exact wind direction by the compass and his opinion about a possible change in direction during the day.

Only people who are very close to nature can do this. City people, I suppose, have all this done for them by the weatherman on the radio. It is not possible to be in Ireland for long without realising that the weather is a constant topic of conversation. This may be due to the Irish climate's unpredictable behaviour. A soft day, or *lá bog*, in Gaelic, is a lovely phrase and, like *lá breá*, a 'fine' or 'good day', it has become a form of salutation – so much so, that in one Gaelic-speaking area in Munster, tourists were nicknamed '*lá Breás*', not because they arrived with the fine weather, but because *lá breá* was the only Gaelic phrase they knew and constantly practised.

Many people like watching the gentle rain fall and find it therapeutic. I, for one, much enjoy being out *in* the rain. A 'soft day' does not mean that it is actually raining but it does mean that it has rained and is likely to do so again. The rain has a softening effect. As though it has taken the edge off the elements: earth and air are now relaxed and fresh. 'A soft day, thank God!' – because, for so many reasons, the rain is a blessing and has long been regarded as such.

I Wish I Had The Shepherd's Lamb

I wish I had the shepherd's lamb, the shepherd's lamb, the shepherd's lamb, I wish I had the shepherd's lamb and Katie coming after.

CHORUS   *Is Ó! goirim, goirim thú,*
Is grá mo chroí gan cheilg thú,
Is Ó! goirim, goirim thú.
'S tú peata beag do mháithir.

I wish I had the yellow cow, the yellow cow, the yellow cow,
I wish I had the yellow cow, and welcome from my darling.

CHORUS

I wish I had a Kerry cow, a Kerry cow, a Kerry cow,
I wish I had a Kerry cow, I'd milk her night and morning.

CHORUS

I wish I had a Galway hat, a Galway hat, a Galway hat,
I wish I had a Galway hat, I'd give it to my darling.

CHORUS

I wish I had a herd of kine, a herd of kine, a herd of kine,
I wish I had a herd of kine, and Katie from her father.

CHORUS

The chorus translated reads: And O I call you, I call you. You are my heart's love without deceit . . . and you are mother's little pet.

'I Wish I Had The Shepherd's Lamb' is one of those songs most children in Ireland learn at school. Herbert Hughes claims that it is originally from the Glens of Antrim but that it's pretty well-known all over Ireland in both Gaelic and English. Some verses were collected by George Petrie in County Clare early in the last century. The Kerry cow and the Galway hat verses are not in the Hughes version and, for all I know, may have been added by Seán Óg himself, who taught them to me. It is possible that each locality added its own familiar item to the verses to make the song more relevant for the children. The handsome black wide-brimmed hat of the Galway men has been immortalised in the woodcuts of Jack B. Yeats.

An Maidrin Rua

1. *Ag gabháil aduaith dhom thar Sliabh*
      Luachra,
   'Gus mise a cur tuairisc mo ghéanna,
   Ar mo chasa anuas 'sea fuaireas a
      dtuairisc,
   Go raibh maidrín rua dá maoracht.

CHORUS   *An maidrín rua, rua, rua, rua, rua,*
         An maidrín rua tá grána,
         An maidrín rua 'na lui sa luachra,
         'Gus barr a dhá chluais anáirde.

2. 'Good morrow, fox, Good morrow,
      Sir,
   Pray what is that you're eating?'
   'A fine fat goose I stole from you,
   And won't you come and taste it?'
   'O, no indeed, *ní áil lion í,*
   Ni bhlaisead pioc di ar aon chor,
   But I vow and swear you'll dearly
      pay,
   For my fat goose you're eating.'

CHORUS

3. Hark, hark, find her, Lily and Piper
   Cruinnigí na gadhair le na chéile;
   Hark, hark, Trueman, *ta leisce orm*
      cuma,
   Is maith an fear cú thú Bateman.

CHORUS

4. *Tallyho lé na bhonn, tallyho lé na bhonn,*
   Tallyho lé na bhonn a choileáinin;
   Tallyho lé na bhonn, tallyho lé na bhonn,
   Agus barr a dhá chluais anáirde.

CHORUS

5. *Greada chroi cráite chughad a mhaidrín*
      grána,
   Do rug uaim m'ál brea géanna;
   Mo choilig mora breá, mo chearca bhí go
      háluinn,
   Is mo lachainn beaga b'fearr a bhí in
      Éirinn.

CHORUS

The Little Fox

1. As I was travelling north past Luachra
      mountain
   Seeking information about my geese
   I was told, as I turned to come back,
   That a little fox had got them.

CHORUS   The little red fox, red, red, red,
         red.
         The little red fox which is ugly.
         The little red fox, hiding in the
            heather,
         With the tops of his two ears
            protruding.

2. (After the fox invites the farmer to
      taste his own geese, the farmer
      replies:)
   Oh no indeed, I do not care for it,
   I won't even taste a morsel.

CHORUS

3. (Then the farmer summons his dogs)
   Hark, hark, Finder, Lily and Piper,
   Gather the hounds together;
   Hark, hark, Trueman, I'd hate to lie,
   But Bateman, you're one good
      houndsman

CHORUS

4. Tallyho to his feet, tallyho to his feet,
   After him you pups,
   Tallyho to his feet, tallyho to his feet,
   And the top of his two ears
       protruding.

CHORUS

5. Heart-scald to you, you little ugly
       fox,
   Who snatched my fine gaggle of
       geese,
   My fine big cocks, my hens that were
       beautiful,
   And my little ducklings that were
       finest in Ireland.

The *Maidrín Rua*, literally Little Red Dog, is another name for the fox which is generally referred to as *sionnach* in Gaelic. The fox is an old enemy of the farmer, killing his fowl and often depriving the poorer sections of the community of much-needed sources of food. Foxes made few friends in the past. '*An Maidrín Rua*' is a hunting song about chasing the fox and following the hounds, a very popular sport in the past in many parts of Ireland, which is described by Oscar Wilde in another context as 'the unspeakable in full pursuit of the uneatable'.

It is curious that in the song the farmer addresses the fox in English and the fox answers in the same language, though the rest of the dialogue is in Gaelic. I was intrigued to note that on Aran, the Gaelic-speaking islanders addressed their animals, especially their domestic ones, in English, as if animals understood and responded only to that language. This is also the case in Gaelic-speaking Kerry. In another song, '*Sliabh na mBan*', the sound of the hunt is equated with freedom from oppression and, in the sagas of ancient Ireland, the hunt figures prominently though, in those days, their quarry was the wild boar.

The fox is a favourite animal in folksong, displaying on occasion great wit and humour, even in the face of adversity. One wonders, though, why he is often described as crafty, when he is invariably caught.

Óró Mo Bháidín

Crochfaidh mé seólta 'gus gabhfaidh mé siar,
Óró mo churraichín ó,
'S go hoiche Fhéile Eoin ní thiochfaidh mé
    aniar,
Óró mo bháidín.

CHORUS   Óró mo churraichín ó, óró mo
    bháidín
Óró mo churraichín ó, óró mo bháidín

'Snach breá í mo bháidín a' snámh ar an
    gcuan,
Óró mo churraichín ó,
'S na céaslaí a dtarraint go láidir 's go buan,
Óró mo bháidín,

CHORUS

'S nach éachtach a léimreach thar tonntracha
    árd,
Óró mo churraichín ó,
'S nach éatrom í iompar aníos thar an trá
Óró mo bháidín.

CHORUS

Óró my Little Boat

1. I shall hoist sail and go west,
    Óró my little coracle,
    And until Saint John's Eve I shall
        not return,
    Óró my little boat.

CHORUS   Óró my little coracle,
        óró my little boat
    Óró my little coracle,
        óró my little boat

2. Isn't my little boat lovely floating on
        the harbour,
    Óró my little boat,
    And with the oars being pulled strongly
        and steadfastly,
    Óró my little boat.

CHORUS

3. Doesn't she leap blithely over the
        high waves?
    Óró my little boat;
    And isn't she light to carry up on
        the strand?
    Óró my little boat.

CHORUS

'*Óró* my Little Boat' is a fisherman's song in praise of his little boat called the currach which has been used as a means of transport and for fishing along the west coast of Ireland since time immemorial. In Gaelic the word *currach* also means 'unsteady' and, in unskilled hands, this round-bottomed keel-less canoe is anything but steady. The currach is a frail-looking wooden-ribbed craft, covered with canvas and then tarred. It is rowed with bladeless paddles. The canvas has replaced the skins of more ancient times and, as well as waterproofing the canvas, the tar makes it possible to repair quickly and easily any tear in the boat's skin. It is an ideal form of sea transport for the people living along the rugged coastline of western Ireland, especially in places not having safe harbours. Two men can easily pull a currach out of the breakers and carry it on their shoulders over the rocks to the safety of a field. In skilled hands the currach is virtually unsinkable and astonishingly manoeuvrable, most desirable qualities in the unpredictable and often savage Atlantic waves. Accidents, however, do occur, and with tragic consequences. J. M. Singe's play *Riders to the Sea* is built around such a theme. In Kerry a currach is called a *naomhóg* which indicates that this song must come from Connacht – Aran, Connemara or Mayo.

I first reached Inishere strand in a currach, having been transferred from a Connemara hooker a short distance off shore. My husband had reached Inishere a year previously by similar means. He rowed the eleven miles from Kilronan on Inishmore, an experience that he greatly enjoyed as the following extract from a letter he wrote to me at the time clearly shows. The Saint John's Night (Mid-summer night) mentioned in the song is Bonfire Night, a festive occasion that not even a lively boat could tempt a fisherman to miss.

24 August 1953

. . . Looking across the inlet I saw that two men were putting their currach into the water. It was about 7.15. I went quickly to pick up my rucksack and yelled across to them to wait. In a few minutes I was there, asking if they would take me. We agreed on ten shillings. The man in the forward end of the currach was the elder, about forty-five, and was the one to whom I addressed myself. He asked me if I could row. I said yes and was quickly at the middle pair of oars and we were on our way. I had no trouble getting the knack of the oars, imitating the young man in front of me. Soon I was being complimented on my ability to pull. A young girl, perhaps fourteen or fifteen, sat in the stern with her feet folded under her. Her grey eyes and sternly handsome face presented me with a pleasant compendium of the sea, the receding island, setting sun, and the sky, to which she was the foreground.

They spoke an Irish softer than I had heard before. Occasionally the old man would interrogate me as to my nationality and my potential financial status. He seemed impressed with my rowing or at least he let

on that he did in order to get me to row even harder. I did row hard and was quite pleased with myself and with the whole scene about me. The old man's often reiterated phrase of approbation was 'good man, good man', to which my response was to increase the energy of my strokes. 'Ah, man, dear, if I was a girl, I'd fall in love with you,' he would say. 'You're the nicest man I ever know.' 'Do you see that?' he asked. I turned as I leaned back on the oar and couldn't see what he meant. 'No,' I said. He spat into the water. I watched the spittle trail away. 'The sea. And that to her,' he said. There was no mood of propitiation in that man, I thought, the sea's his enemy.

The distance, they said, from Kilronan to Inishere is ten miles. It took us two hours to row it. Except for some slight blisters on my hands, I arrived none the worse for the effort. After pulling the currach up the beach with the help of a number of bystanders, my two companions and a third man who had joined us on the beach made straight for the pub. . . .

R. SELIG

'A man who is not afraid of the sea will soon be drownded,' an Arran Islander once told Synge, 'for he will be going out on a day he shouldn't. But we do be afraid of the sea, and we do only be drownded now and again.'

Báidín Fheilimí　Phelimy's Little Boat

Báidín Fheilimí d'imigh go Góla,	Phelimy's boat went to Gola,
Báidín Fheilimí 's Feilimí ann	Phelimy's boat and Phelimy in it.
Báisín Fheilimí d'imigh go Góla,	Phelimy's boat went to Gola,
Báidín Fheilimí 's Feilimí ann	Phelimy's boat and Phelimy in it.

CHORUS　*Báidín bídeach, báidín beósach,*　　　CHORUS　The little boat, the lively boat,
　　　　　Báidín bóidheach, báidín Fheilimí,　　　　　　The charming boat, Phelimy's boat;
　　　　　Báidín díreach, báidín deóntach,　　The straight boat, the willing boat,
　　　　　Báidín Fheilimí 's Feilimí ann.　　Phelimy's boat and Phelimy in it.

Báidín Fheilimí d'imigh go Tóraí,	Phelimy's boat went to Tory,
Báidín Fheilimí 's Feilimí ann.	Phelimy's boat and Phelimy in it.
Báidín Fheilimí d'imigh go Tóraí,	Phelimy's boat went to Tory,
Báidín Fheilimí 's Feilimí ann.	Phelimy's boat and Phelimy in it.

CHORUS　　　　　　　　　　　　　　　　CHORUS

Báidín Fheilimí brisiú i dTóraí,	Phelimy's boat was wrecked in Tory,
Báidín Fheilimí 's Feilimí ann.	Phelimy's boat and Phelimy in it.
Báidín Fheilimí brisiú i dTóraí,	Phelimy's boat was wrecked in Tory,
Báidín Fheilimí 's Feilimí ann.	Phelimy's boat and Phelimy in it.

CHORUS　　　　　　　　　　　　　　　　CHORUS

Báidín Fheilimí filleadh tránóna,	Phelimy's boat returned at evening time,
Iasc ar bórd 's Feilimí ann.	Fish on board and Phelimy too.
Báidín Fheilimi filleadh tránóna,	Phelimy's boat returned at evening time,
Iasc ar bórd 's Feilimí ann.	Fish on board and Phelimy too.

CHORUS　　　　　　　　　　　　　　　　CHORUS

'Báidín Fheilimí' is a song in the same vein as '*Óró Mo Bháidín*', except that in this case the location is Tory Island off the Donegal coast in the north of Ireland. I do enjoy the last verse, the Resurrection verse, because such a nice little boat should not be allowed to remain shipwrecked for long. Even the fish got back in! In folk-song, such verses are regarded as 'ghost' verses. Phelimy had been drowned and what we are seeing is his phantom. Fishermen everywhere possess a tradition of 'ghost vessels' – boats which appear at sea and are regarded either as a kind of premonition of disaster or a confirmation of a disaster already happened. Walter Macken, the very popular Galway novelist and playwright, has written a chilling description of one of these spectral boats off the Galway coast in his book *Rain On The Wind*.

The Meeting of the Waters

1. There is not in the wide world a
       valley so sweet
   As that vale in whose bosom the
       bright waters meet!
   Oh! the last rays of feeling and life
       must depart
   Ere the bloom of that valley shall fade
       from my heart.

2. Yet it *was* not that nature had shed
       o'er the scene
   Her purest of crystal and brightest of
       green;
   'Twas *not* the soft magic of streamlet
       or hill,
   Oh! no – it was something more
       exquisite still.

3. 'Twas that friends, the beloved of my
       bosom, were near,
   Who made every dear scene of
       enchantment more dear,
   And who felt how the best charms of
       nature improve,
   When we see them reflected from
       looks that we love.

4. Sweet vale of Avoca! how calm could
       I rest
   In thy bosom of shade with the
       friends I love best,
   Where the storms that we feel in this
       cold world should cease,
   And our hearts, like thy waters, be
       mingled in peace!

Croagh Patrick, locally known as 'The Reek' is Ireland's holy mountain. It rises 2,510 feet from the shore of Clew Bay. Tradition has it that Saint Patrick fasted on top of this mountain during the Lent of the year 441 and from time immemorial Reek Sunday (the last Sunday in July) finds hundreds of pilgrims climbing the reek to hear Mass at the tiny windswept church at the top. Some people do this penitential pilgrimage every year.

In a note accompanying his song, Thomas Moore had this to say: '"The Meeting of the Waters" forms a part of that beautiful scenery which lies between Rathdrum and Arklow, in the county of Wicklow, and these lines were suggested by a visit to this romantic spot in the summer of the year 1807.' In fact, this place is just south of Rathdrum where the Avonmore and Avonbeg Rivers meet the Avoca River, a magnificent view overlooked by Castle Howard. Nearby is what is known as Thomas Moore's tree, where the poet is reputed to have spent many hours in meditation, but, sadly, it is now cordoned off to protect it against souvenir-hunters.

The entire Vale of Avoca, indeed the whole of mountainous County Wicklow, is exceptionally beautiful. Not far away is picturesque Glendalough (The Glen of the Two Lakes) with its sixth-century monastic ruins and eleventh-century round tower. Saint Kevin, who died in 618 founded this famous monastery.

For a time Glendalough was one of the four pilgrimage centres of Ireland, the other three being Downpatrick, where the saint is buried, Croagh Patrick in County Mayo, where the saint once fasted and did vigil, and St Patrick's Purgatory, an island on Lough Derg in County Donegal. The last two places are still used as places of pilgrimage and, as a young widow, I made the three-day pilgrimage to Lough Derg, as it is generally called. This serious penitential exercise seems to have changed little since the Middle Ages, when it attracted high-ranking pilgrims from all over Europe. Even then it was reputed to be a 'tough' pilgrimage with its fasting, walking barefoot over the stony 'penitential beds' and the lack of sleep. Even Dante made particular mention of the place as a very strict pilgrimage.

I found it difficult enough picking my footsteps over the sharp stones but it became doubly difficult when an old man, deep in his devotions and oblivious of his surroundings, decided to latch on to me and lean on my shoulder for support. With a stick in one hand and his other hand supported on my shoulder, the pair of us – complete strangers to each other – walked around the 'beds' together in silence, without ever exchanging as much as an introduction.

Among Silence

Where bubbles dawdle green wands wave
And tadpoles jerk,
Where slow pond water slowly scurling flows
Seeming still,
The sky and half the meadow mirrored,
And moderate nature rests in pond-side reeds,
Drowses in the meadow, dreams in water volumes.
Everywhere one looks tranquillity does soothe the gaze.
Peace placates the wild senses and
Truth lies sleeping.
Look down into the pond
Change your element.
Let fancy take you. Plunge down.
Your ear cannot hear, your lungs dare not stir,
Yet the blood buzzes.
Fancy feeds your air, your eyes are clear.
You swim among silence in a green world.

'Among Silence' is the last poem my husband Richard Selig wrote. It had no title and he intended to make it much longer. After Richard's death, when I set the piece to music, I decided to call it 'Among Silence'. Sometimes, when I find myself alone in an Irish meadow or wood on a drowsy summer's day, this song comes drifting into my mind.

One of the things that struck me most forcibly when I 'came out' after twelve and a half years of monastic seclusion was the concerted assault, virtually from all sides, on silence. No matter where one travelled – in planes, in lifts, shopping centres, hotels, restaurants, sometimes even in streets – there was the inescapable piped music and, most undemocratically of all, there was no freedom of choice and no escaping it. Personally, I have at times a need for silence and I treasure and try to make use of the opportunity when it presents itself, to 'soak in' silence. These, what I call, 'oases of silence' whether inner or outer, are healing and reviving. They help one to become more receptive, more aware.

I remember an occasion when my harp was standing in my cottage near an open window on an exquisitely quiet, very sunny summer's day. Stillness all round except for the occasional sounds of nature outside the window, which never interfere with silence as far as I'm concerned. Then gradually I became aware of the most distant though distinct sound of very sweet music. Greatly puzzled it took me some moments to realise that the sound was coming from the harp: a gentle breeze had touched the strings. Thinking about this incident afterwards, I saw an analogy there with how the Holy Spirit must sometimes work. Inspiration of all sorts must need a certain amount of quiet.

There is a rather special kind of charged silence about some of our more ancient prehistoric places and ruins in Ireland or indeed anywhere. There is, too, a refreshing silence to be found in the lonelier more remote rural areas of the country. For me, few outdoor pleasures can surpass a bicycle ride along the byroads and country lanes of Ireland or in the more rugged areas like Donegal, Connemara or Kerry. I know Donegal and Connemara reasonably well and I once spent a most pleasant week in Dunquin in County Kerry after my final examination at boarding school in Dublin.

I joined my sister Joan for a holiday in the Dingle peninsula. Joan, like every other member of the Dublin Abbey Theatre at the time, was obliged to freshen up her Gaelic by spending part of the summer in some Gaeltacht (Gaelic-speaking area) or other. It was a lovely holiday and we spent most of our days out on bicycles. I remember sensing air laden with the sweet-honeyed scent of the whins and the sight of the deep yellow flower and the red of the fuschia was a delight to the eye.

On one of our excursions we visited Gallarus Oratory, one of the best-preserved early Christian church buildings in the country. Built entirely of unmortared stone, with corbelled roofing, after over a thousand years it's a wonder that it is still completely weatherproof. Little did I know then as we examined and crept in and out of this oratory, that one day, in the not too distant future, I too would be following the monastic rule, though not in Ireland or in a stone hut.

OPPOSITE *Dunquin, County Kerry. Gaelic is still the language of this district as it was of the nearby Blasket Islands now uninhabited since 1953. It was the Blaskets that produced such well known classics as* Twenty Years a Growing *(O'Sullivan) and* The Island Man *(O'Crohan).*

Gogaí-Ó-Gaog

Agus gogaí-ó-gaog! Cá ndéanfad mo nead?
Dá ndéanainn sa tsliabh í, gheobhadh na gadhair fiaigh í,
Agus gogaí-ó-gaog! Cá ndéanfad mo nead?

Agus gogaí-ó-gaog! Cá ndéanfad mo nead?
Dá ndéanainn sa trá i gheobhadh na faoileáin í.
Agus gogaí-ó-gaog! Cá ndéanfad mo nead?

Dá ndéanainn sa tuí í gheobhadh na leanaí í.

Dá ndéanainn sa chruaich í gheobhadh a' Bhean Rua í.

Dá ndéanainn sa ghleann i gheobhadh a' Fear Cam í.

Dá ndéanainn sa choill í gheobhadh buachaill na ngadhar í.

Dá ndéanainn sa chlai í gheobhadh a' caistin í,
Agus ní fheadar in Éirinn cá ndéanfad mo nead.

Gogaí-Ó-Gaog

'Gogaí-ó-gaog' is the sound a bird makes to attract attention. Each verse starts with a complaint and ends with a complaint by asking where on earth can she make her nest? *'Gogaí-ó-gaog, where shall I make my nest?'*

If I should make my nest on the hillside, the hunting hounds would find it;

If I should make it on the strand, the seagulls would find it;

If I should make it in the hay, the children would find it;

If I should make it in the turf-bank, the Red Woman would find it;

If I should make it in the glen, the Crooked Man would find it;

If I should make it in the wood, the houndsman would find it;

If I should make it in the fence, the flatter-stone would find it;

And I don't know under heaven where shall I make it.

'Gogaí-ó-gaog', on the face of it, appears to be about a bird worrying about where to make her nest. But one can apply the theme to any distracted person fretting about something they have to do and making endless excuses about the difficulty of positive action. Nothing ventured, nothing gained, and for those who look hard enough, there are hazards attached to any kind of activity, even to inactivity. The bird in this song was crossing her bridges before she ever met them and probably ended up making no nest at all.

The Queen of Connemara

Oh! my boat can swiftly float
In the teeth of wind and weather,
And outsail the fastest hooker
Between Galway and Kinsale.
When the white rim of the ocean
And the wild waves rush together –
Oh, she rides in her pride
Like a seabird in a gale

CHORUS   She's neat, oh, she's sweet;
She's a beauty in every line –
The Queen of Connemara
Is this bounding barque of mine.

When she's loaded down with fish.
'Til the water lips the gunwale,
Not a drop she'll take aboard her
That would wash a fly away;
From the fleet she speeds out quickly
Like a greyhound from her kennel.
'Till she lands her silvery store the first
On old Kinvara Quay.

*A Connemara Hooker loading turf for the Aran
Islands. Sixty years ago there were hundreds of these
sailing boats trading between the towns, coastal
villages and islands off the west coast of Ireland. The
coming of bottled gas to Aran removed the last
practical excuse for their existence and few now
remain.*

'The Queen of Connemara' belonged to a unique class of sailing vessels known in Ireland as Connemara or Galway hookers. The hooker, as we know the boat today, has been in use in the west of Ireland since the seventeenth century and is thought to have been based on the design of a Dutch sailing vessel, probably shipwrecked in Irish waters a couple of centuries ago. Hookers were used for ferrying turf, people and other cargo between coastal towns and between the islands and the mainland. The last worthwhile work of the boats was ferrying turf from Connemara to the Aran islands but the advent of bottled gas to the islands ended that trade and made the Connemara hooker redundant, and it became almost extinct. Only a few of those sailing boats now remain – reconditioned and collectors' items, relics of bygone days.

The song builds a nostalgic picture of one of these boats, the *Queen of Connemara*, attributing to her poetic qualities which, unfortunately, these hookers never had! I remember seeing several of these boats sailing across Galway Bay bringing turf to Aran. Halfway through our honeymoon, my late husband and I, as I have mentioned before, sailed to Inishere on one. The *Dun Aengus*, the regular Galway–Aran steamer was not sailing and we were advised to go to

Carraroe and sail in a hooker. We left the harbour at Carraroe at 8 a.m. to sail across a very smooth sea, and I still remember with delight the taste of the strong sweet tea that the *bádóir* (boatman) served us when we were out in the middle of the bay. It was brewed on a turf fire somewhere in the prow of the boat and served with chunks of buttered bread, which the boatman shared with us as his boat sluggishly tacked to and fro on the sparkling waters of Galway Bay. Somewhat less enjoyable is the memory of almost falling overboard into that sparkling ocean when the old *bádóir* suddenly thrust a large squirming fish in my direction, frightening me out of my wits. He hadn't realised that a landlubber could be so fearful of the fish he had just plucked from the sea. It took us many hours to reach Inishere, and whenever I hear mention of 'The Queen of Connemara' my mind goes back to that memorable day.

The words of 'The Queen of Connemara' are by Francis A. Fahy and the music is by Alica A. Needham.

Broadly speaking, 'nature' can generally mean the face of the land, the elements therein. These, together with the language, history and philosophy of life of a people, play a vital role in providing the overarching canopy of symbols that forge the consciousness of a nation. Believing that somewhere there is a place one can call home seems to be a psychological need in people. Hankering after 'my territory', 'mon pays', or the more fashionable 'roots' is a frequent preoccupation in the literature and song of exiles. The Irish have been going into exile for centuries – so much so that today only a small fraction of the Irish people inhabit the island of Ireland (24.4% of the population of the USA claim Irish ancestry). I think it appropriate therefore to conclude this book with an exile song called 'The Quiet Land of Érin'.

Chapter IX

The Quiet Land of Érin

1. By myself I'd be in Árdaí Chuain
   Where the mountain stands away;
   And 'tis I would let the Sunday go
   In the cuckoo's glen above the bay.

   CHORUS   *Agus och, och Éire 'lig is ó,*
                Éire liondubh is ó,
           Ah, the quiet land of Érin.

2. Ah, my heart is weary all alone,
   And it sends a lonely cry
   To the land that sings beyond my
       dreams.
   And the lonely Sundays passed
       me by.

   CHORUS

3. I would ravel back the twisted years
   In the bitter wasted winds,
   If the God above would let me lie
   In a quiet place above the whins.

   CHORUS

'The Quiet Land' is a translation of '*Ardaí Chuain*', a Gaelic poem written by the Antrim poet, Mac Ambróis, during a spell of enforced exile in Scotland. Exile is a condition well-known to many people from Ireland. Few countries can have been more riven with strife and war than our small and ancient island. Innumerable ruined monasteries and castles that scar and yet enhance the land bear witness to the destruction that can be the fruit of unbridled hatred, greed and revenge, in times of war and, supposedly, peace. The surrounding waters too, the sometimes intemperate Atlantic, can savage the coastline and tear apart the hearts of those it leaves bereaved. And yet there is also a great quietness about Ireland. Perhaps it can be likened to the inner stillness of someone who, having suffered beyond all telling, has emerged with trust intact.

For centuries Irish men and women have been leaving the shores of their country, voluntarily and from necessity, so that there are more Irish people outside the country than in it. Many of these regard themselves as exiles, in the wider sense of that word, despite frequent return visits, and they carry with them in their hearts wherever they go the secrets of the hillsides and the call of the trees and rivers of Ireland. I have met them at my concerts in far distant places.

With so many Irish people abroad, it is not surprising, then, that many of our songs have exile as their theme, and, for that reason, I've decided to end this book with my favourite, *The Quiet Land of Érin*. The translation was made for me by my sister Joan and I used it as a theme song for a BBC television series I had when I was twenty. Despite the turmoil that many associate with Irish history, both past and present, I find myself most at home with the concept of Ireland as the Quiet Land. To my mind, Joan has captured something of the essence of Ireland in that phrase 'The Quiet Land of Érin'.

There are between 30,000 and 40,000 forts to be found in Ireland. They vary in type from the circular ring of earth surrounded by a ditch to the huge stone forts of Aran and Kerry. They date from the Iron Age to early Christian times. The coming of the Normans to Ireland (1169) started a wave of castle building and the earliest examples are fortified mounds and mottes but the commonest surviving form of the Irish Castle is a square stone tower with narrow windows. In the 17th century many of these castles became fortified dwelling houses. Every county in Ireland has its share of ruined castles. For instance, in County Limerick alone there are over a thousand.

Selected Bibliography

BARRY, Phillips, *Irish Come All Ye's*: *Journal of American Folklore*, 1909

BREATHNACH, Breandan, *Ceol Rince Na hÉireann*, Dublin, 1963

BREATHNACH, Breandan, *Folk Music and Dances of Ireland*, Dublin, 1971

CEOL, A. *Journal of Irish Music*, Dublin, in progress

CLANDILLON, Seamus and HANNAGAN, Margaret, *Songs of the Irish Gaels*, O.U.P., London, 1927

COLE, William, *Folk Songs of England, Ireland, Scotland and Wales*, Charles Hausen Music, New York, 1961

CORKERY, Daniel, *The Hidden Ireland*, Gill and MacMillan, 1924

Folk Music Journal, English Folk Dance & Song Society, London, in progress (a continuation of the *Journal of the Folk Song Society*, 1899–1931 and *Journal of the English Folk Dance & Song Society*, 1932–1964)

HARDIMAN, James, *Irish Minstrelsy* (2 volumes), London, 1831; facsimile reprint, Shannon, Irish University Press, 1971

HENRY, Sam, *Songs of the People*, edited by John Moulden, Belfast, 1979

HUGHES, Herbert, *Songs of Uladh* (as Padraig macAodh O Neill), Belfast, 1904

HUGHES, Herbert, *Irish Country Songs* (4 volumes), London, 1909–1936

Irish Folk Music Studies—Éigse Cheol Tíre, Dublin, in progress

Journal of the Irish Folk Song Society (29 volumes), London, 1904–1937

JOYCE, Patrick Weston, *Ancient Music of Ireland*, Dublin, 1912

JOYCE, Patrick Weston, *Old Irish Folk Music and Songs*, Dublin, 1909; facsimile reprint, New York, 1965

KENNEDY, Peter, *Folk Songs of Britain and Ireland*, London, 1975

MAGUIRE, John and Robin Morton, *Come Day, Go Day, God Send Sunday*, London, 1973

MARSHALL, John J., *Popular Rhymes and Sayings of Ireland*, Dungannon, 1931

MORTON, Robin, *Folk Songs Sung in Ulster*, Cork, 1970

Ó BOYLE, Seán, *The Irish Song Tradition*, Dublin, 1976

ODORNO, Theodor W. *Introduction to the Sociology of Music*, Seabury Press, New York, 1976

Ó LOCHLAINN, Colm, *Irish Street Ballads*, Dublin, 1939

Ó LOCHLAINN, Colm, *More Irish Street Ballads*, Dublin, 1965

Old Come All Ye's, The Derry Journal, no date

O'NEILL, Francis, *The Music of Ireland*, Chicago, 1903

O'NEILL, Francis, *Irish Folk Music: A Fascinating Hobby*, Chicago, 1910

O'SULLIVAN, Donal, *Carolan: Life, Times and Music of an Irish Harper*, London (2 volumes), 1958

O'SULLIVAN, Donal, *Songs of the Irish*, Dublin, 1967

Ó TUAMA, Seán, *An Grá in Amhráin na nDaoine*, Dublin, 1960

Ó TUAMA, Seán and KINSELLA, Thomas, *Poems of the Dispossessed*, Dolman Press, Dublin, 1981

Ó TUAMA, Seán Og, *An Choisir Cheoil*, Dublin, 1960

PETRIE, George, *Complete Collection of Irish Music*, London, 1902–5

PETRIE, George, *Ancient Music of Ireland* (2 volumes), Dublin, 1855; facsimile reprint, Gregg International, 1967

RIMMER, Joan, *The Irish Harp*, Dublin, 1977

Treoir (The Magazine of Traditional Music, Song and Dance), Dublin 1968, in progress

Ulster Folklife, Belfast, in progress

WALSH, Patrick, *Songs of the Gael*, Dublin, 1915–1922

WRIGHT, Robert L., *Irish Emigrant Ballads and Songs*, Ohio, 1975

YEATS, Gráinne, *The Belfast Harpers Festival 1792*, Gael-linn Teo., Dublin, 1980

ZIMMERMANN, Georges-Denis, *Songs of Irish Rebellion*, Dublin, 1967

The High Cross of Ahenny, County Tipperary.

A Note on the Structure of Irish Songs

When Edward Bunting began to write down the melodies he had collected from the ten harpers at the Belfast Festival of 11, 12 and 13 July 1792, he found himself in a musical quandary. Had he heard accurately, or were the harpers really playing their tunes in the scales he had first noted down? Whatever his doubts, what he eventually printed could not be played back on the musicians' instruments.

This 'doctoring' of songs and music was to persist among collectors and publishers – and even scholars – for another century. Stanford and others in Ireland, and Cecil Sharp in England, regarded the ethnic musician as a sort of noble savage for whom his native music was an instinctive form of expression. And, while this 'noble savage' was capable of producing music of such charm that larger, more extravagant musical forms might be built upon it, he certainly did not possess the facility for singing in the complex musical scales which were first recognised by Hughes and a handful of others.

Presenting his first notebooks of traditional songs to Stanford, Hughes was told by the composer that it was impossible that untutored singers could sing deliberately far outside the tonic range – the black and white notes of the piano. And yet, Hughes was claiming that these same singers were indeed singing in scales which were as complicated as the Greek modes; in simple terms, they were singing notes which fell somewhere between the piano keys.

Percy French, in one of his comic songs, might have been trying to accompany a traditional singer on the piano when he wrote:

> White notes I found were wrong, so were the black,
> For you had pitched the song right in the crack!

Stanford's retort to Hughes was that these singers 'were only singing out of tune'. But, with the arrival of the recording machine, we have been able to listen to traditional singers from a wide range of countries and cultures, and to come to the inarguable conclusion that a common source applies to folksong and to Plain song. This is a musical form which has a structure based on what we call 'Greek' or 'medieval' modes or scales, of which there are seven, although Irish song, in common with other well-preserved north-European music, is dominated by a profusion of melodies in the sol-, la-, doh- and re-mode scales.

In folksong, we have to remember that we are not dealing exclusively with the tempered scale: what A. L. Lloyd calls 'piano-tuner's music'. Traditional singers' intonations are full of off-centre notes, and these seem to be 'wrong' to the conventionally-trained musician.

Bartok, realising that traditional singers were using complex scales, devised an unsophisticated technique for recording more accurately what he was hearing: to him the five-line stave, which we all use today, was not sufficiently versatile, and so he placed a small arrow above a written note to indicate whether it should be sung a little above or a little below the stave line on which it appeared. His device was copied by many other east-European musicologists.

The Rev. Richard Henebry (*A Handbook of Irish Music, 1928*) submitted a series of phonographically-recorded tunes to tonometric analysis, hoping to define a theory of a set of national Irish autochthonous scales, but failed to convince because of the limited range of his samples and the coarseness of his methods. But he was on the right track. Hughes was right when he said that so-called 'quarter tones' were being used instinctively 'by the unlearned peasant', but both he and Henebry were wrong to think that such a phenomenon was exclusively Irish when it is, in fact, universal.

To Hughes, the domestic piano was a compromise in tuning, and folksongs set for the piano were also a compromise. Cecil Sharp set the first song he ever collected, 'The Seeds of Love', and played it back on the piano to its singer, who failed to recognise it! Hughes and Henebry were also right in thinking that the piano had no legitimate place in the practice or cultivation of folk music. Emanuel Moór (1863–1931) nearly came to the rescue when he invented the twin-keyboard Duplex-Coupler piano, a machine capable of playing quarter-tones, but his invention is now an obscure musical eccentricity.

'The structure of Irish music,' Hughes said in a 1933 lecture, 'has represented an insuperable barrier to proper publication. The tunes are unprintable in our modern notation, and the barrier is the scale of the domestic piano.'

Two more examples of the vagaries of traditional music will suffice to illustrate what a rocky path you must tread if you wish to understand the nature of Irish – or other – music solely from the printed page; and both examples are reflections of Sharp's experiences with the singer of 'The Seeds of Love'.

Henebry, a skilled fiddle-player, who admitted no formal musical qualification, gave a tune to Hughes who immediately played it back to him on the piano. To Hughes' astonishment, Henebry replied: 'I cannot hear that; it means nothing to me.' The tempered scale of the piano had confused the ear of the man who had been accustomed to the free-ranging fiddle and voice of the country musician, and, as Hughes admitted, 'the addition of harmony only added to his bewilderment!'

At about this same time, Hughes heard a young man in County Antrim playing the tune associated with Moore's 'Minstrel Boy' on a uillean pipe chanter, and it was Hughes' turn to be bewildered.

Doolough bog in County Mayo. Chatting to turfcutters, Jim and John. Turf (or peat) is still the only source of heat in many houses in the remoter parts of rural Ireland and there is nothing cosier than to sit before a big turf fire on a rainy day in a part of the country where there is no shortage of either.

It was a wonderfully beautiful distortion of the melody: like, but unlike. And the primitive form incomparably better. I felt like some early Christian apostle to whom a great light has been suddenly revealed; whereas I was simply stumbling on the fact that our native music has as much relationship to the 'well-tempered clavier' of Sebastian Bach as Gaelic has to Cockney. When we listen to our music in terms of modern harmonic practice, however lovely and imaginative it may be, we are listening to an art that has been compromised.

JOHN PADDY BROWNE